"Triple Fit Strategy works! In fact, it has become embedded in the way we manage our relationships to stay close to our strategic customers, regardless of industry conditions."

—**VINCENT CLERC**, CEO, A.P. Moller – Maersk

"*Triple Fit Strategy* vividly illustrates how companies—sellers and buyers—can build a business relationship as though they belong to one company. The book shows how to achieve 'three fits' between them at the planning, execution, and resource levels. It's a must-read, filled with insightful and interesting examples."

—**W. CHAN KIM**, Professor of Strategy and Codirector, Blue Ocean Strategy Institute, INSEAD; eight-time Thinkers50 award winner; and bestselling coauthor, *Blue Ocean Strategy, Beyond Disruption*, and *Blue Ocean Shift*

"*Triple Fit Strategy* has started to transform our customer interactions. We now engage more in strategic dialogues focused on joint value creation, as if we were one company."

—**NIELS PÖRKSEN**, CEO, Südzucker Group

"*Triple Fit Strategy* is smart, practical, and based on the authors' years of experience across industries. It can help you turn customer focus from rhetoric to reality."

—**FRANK CESPEDES**, Senior Lecturer of Business Administration, Harvard Business School; author, *Sales Management That Works* and *Aligning Strategy and Sales*

"Rarely does one encounter the right mix of conceptual sales strategy, hands-on tactics, and empirically proven bottom-line impact. *Triple Fit Strategy* stands out as an exception—a must-read for business leaders and their sales teams."

—**THOMAS GØGSIG**, Chief Commercial Officer, ECCO Group

"Triple Fit Strategy helps us to develop high-value relationships with our customers and project partners and run them like a business."

—**MICHAEL DOBLER**, Head of Global Account Management, Schindler

"Two companies working as if they were one is the motto this book brings to life. It helps you realize game-changer ideas, based on a joint vision, as we did with Walmart."

—**TOM MUCCIO**, former President, Global Customer Teams, Procter & Gamble

"*Triple Fit Strategy* aligns business objectives to create a true win-win relationship. The process steps are easy to implement and lead to mutual business success."

—**YVES ROGIVUE**, Global CEO, Indicia Worldwide

"In business there is nothing more satisfying than cocreating value for customers, and in so doing, creating value for employees, value for stakeholders, and value for the planet. I have used the Triple Fit canvas, and it works brilliantly."

—**MALCOLM McDONALD**, Professor Emeritus of Marketing, Cranfield University School of Management; author, *Marketing Plans: How to Prepare Them, How to Use Them*

"*Triple Fit Strategy* addresses how companies can recognize and overcome the barriers to strategic alignment with their major customers. Based on rigorous research and decades of work with companies, this book is a must-read for anyone who serves customers, from the CEO on down."

—**GEORGE S. YIP,** Emeritus Professor of Marketing and Strategy, Imperial College Business School, London; coauthor, *Managing Global Customers*

"Triple Fit methodology has helped to deepen our partnerships with our customers as we strive to achieve our mutual growth ambitions. If you want to create lasting customer relationships, read this book."

—**SANJAY VASUDEVAN**, Global Commercial Head, Key Accounts, A.P. Moller - Maersk

"*Triple Fit Strategy* is a valuable resource for business professionals, providing a clear and practical strategy framework with many real-world examples. The book's straightforward advice and engaging use of metaphors help readers make better decisions, build strong relationships, and achieve growth in their businesses."

> —**RAINER STERN**, Global Vice President, Sales Acceleration and Leadership, SAP

"Our historical data proves that using the techniques associated with relationship selling, learned through the Triple Fit method and the value creation process, results in hit rates above fifty percent. When we bid on projects with no relationship management instead providing only a price/plan proposal, our success rate drops to below twenty percent"

> —**DREW TOPHAM**, Senior Director, Global Major Projects, Otis Elevator Company

"The Triple Fit canvas helped us to effectively develop a 360° view of our business relationships, align business strategies across products and geographies, and cocreate value with our top customers."

> —**MICHAEL HEUER**, former CEO, Roche Diagnostics

"Presenting my Triple Fit findings to my customers has led to more open conversations regarding budgetary planning and alignment of resources."

> —**STEPHEN COLGAN**, Senior Account Director, Oracle; former Global Client Partner, Vodafone

"With the help of the Triple Fit Strategy, I identified $25 million of savings per day in my customer's value chain. I am now acting as the conductor of a compelling global value proposition."

> —**CHRISTINE DICKSON**, Global Key Client Director, A.P. Moller - Maersk

"The Triple Fit canvas enabled us to engage successfully with 3M's diverse technology network. It was also instrumental in creating a sustainable project pipeline that will help bring new products rapidly to market and accelerate growth."

—**ALAN WEINSTEIN**, Director of Customer Experience, BASF

"The Triple Fit canvas is a very intuitive tool. It's not an additional task but the essential basis to continuously cocreate value with our most important customers."

—**MATTHIAS KIESSLING**, Head of Global Business Services, Konica Minolta Business Solutions Europe

"The Triple Fit tool for developing business partnerships is transformative, streamlining collaboration. Its innovative features enhance communication, align goals, and foster trust, driving mutual growth and long-term success. An indispensable asset, Triple Fit propels partnerships to new heights."

—**NICOLAS SEEGMULLER**, Global Account Director, AGRANA Fruit

"*Triple Fit Strategy* is the game changer that allowed us to reinvent the conversation and future engagement with our customers."

—**MOSHE LOBERANT**, Director, Global Key Accounts, A.P. Moller - Maersk

"Triple Fit is the perfect framework that has allowed us to stop pushing for solutions and products and start understanding our customers' goals and where they want to be."

—**JOSEFINA GODOY LEMOS**, Cased Goods Sales Head, Chile and Argentina, Hillebrand Gori

"*Triple Fit Strategy* has helped us orchestrate business projects with our strategic customers by collaborating effectively to take the relationship to the next level. It can help you change the game in your customer relationships."

—**ARIANE HELMBRECHT**, Regional Business Director, Europe, Evonik

"What I like most about *Triple Fit Strategy* is that it helps to reveal not only our areas for improvement but also those on the client's side, thus outlining a common strategy for our joint growth. This requires effort from both sides, but it brings us from supplier-customer level to partner-partner level."

— **HANNA KOVAL**, Client Success Manager, Global Business Services, Konica Minolta Business Solutions Europe

"The Triple Fit Strategy aligns multiple stakeholders and objectives in an orchestrated manner and elevates even complex relationships into a more strategic, sustainable dialogue. It is intuitive, agile, and considers context, perspective, and business dimensions. 1+1=3!"

— **CHRISTIAN DOGANER**, Strategic Transformation Director, Indicia Worldwide

"The Triple Fit Strategy is a game changer, delivering strategic alignment that drives revenue growth, cost reduction, and innovation. In my experience, it transforms customer relationships and processes, showing tangible results and unlocking new potential within six months."

— **NICOLAAS SMIT**, Key Account Management Consultant and Interim Manager, Rebelution; Visiting Fellow, Strategic Sales Leadership, Cranfield School of Management, Cranfield, England

"A must-read for sales and procurement teams alike, *Triple Fit Strategy* offers a joint, pragmatic, road-map approach to sustainable value creation, driving business success and competitive advantage along the value chain."

— **SIGRID BRENDEL**, founder and Strategic Adviser, Brendel Interim; former Chief Procurement Officer, Campari Group

TRIPLE
FIT
STRATEGY

TRIPLE
FIT
STRATEGY

HOW TO BUILD LASTING
CUSTOMER RELATIONSHIPS
AND BOOST GROWTH

CHRISTOPH SENN
MEHAK GANDHI

HARVARD BUSINESS REVIEW PRESS
BOSTON, MASSACHUSETTS

Library of Congress Cataloging-in-Publication Data

Names: Senn, Christoph, 24 April 1963-, author. | Gandhi, Mehak, author.
Title: Triple fit strategy : how to build lasting customer relationships
    and boost growth / Christoph Senn and Mehak Gandhi.
Description: Boston, Massachusetts : Harvard Business Review Press, [2024] |
    Includes index. |
Identifiers: LCCN 2024011593 (print) | LCCN 2024011594 (ebook) |
    ISBN 9781647827144 (hardcover) | ISBN 9781647827151 (epub)
Subjects: LCSH: Industrial marketing. | Value. | Customer relations.
Classification: LCC HF5415.1263 .S48 2024 (print) | LCC HF5415.1263
    (ebook) | DDC 658.8/04—dc23/eng/20240709
LC record available at https://lccn.loc.gov/2024011593
LC ebook record available at https://lccn.loc.gov/2024011594

ISBN: 978-1-64782-714-4
eISBN: 978-1-64782-715-1

To my wife, Eva, and our children, Michelle, David, and Markus. You constantly inspire me to build lasting personal and business relationships. And to you, dear reader, for aspiring to become a true value creator and get closer to your customers than ever before.
—Christoph

To my parents, Harish and Seema, for guiding my journey with your unconditional love, and my sister, Prerna, for sharing with me a childhood filled with the many joys of reading books. And to the ones reading this, may the power of words inspire your dreams.
—Mehak

CONTENTS

ORCHESTRATING MUTUAL GROWTH

Today's business customers don't just buy products and services; they buy expectations. Yet, even the best price at superior performance is only considered table stakes. What these customers want is the commitment of and access to the supplier's total operations. They want problem-solving and creative thinking to keep their business ahead of competition. They want partners.

Compare this view to listening to a symphony orchestra—you expect a seamless performance from the entire orchestra. To achieve this, the conductor plays a critical role, even though a symphony is an auditory experience, and the conductor doesn't make a sound. Still, his or her role is critical in connecting the different sections of the orchestra that cannot all hear each other.

Customer relationships benefit from orchestration efforts. But it's not just about growing your own business as a seller. It's about orchestrating mutual growth, that starts with growing your customer's business. In our research, we have found that only 15 percent of frontline sellers meet these expectations. Members of that group double their business in three years, on average, while other approaches suppliers take are stagnant or achieve only moderate growth. Similarly, our research has shown that only 14 percent of senior managers have adopted the customer-centric perspective and behavior required to orchestrate better partnerships with customers. It's worth it to become more like this 14 percent: these growth champions increase sales and profitability at twice the rate of their peers.

What is the reason for such a discrepancy in growth and profitability? Our research evidence shows that successful companies move beyond the typical product-market fit type of sales approach to what we call "Triple Fit Strategy." Instead of mainly promoting the value proposition of a product or service, Triple Fit Strategy seeks to achieve, as its name suggests, three fits between sellers and buyers at the planning, execution, and resource levels. At the heart of Triple Fit Strategy is a simple question: "What if we—supplier and customer— were one company?" Answering this question will establish a shared language, leading to a blueprint for mutual growth at scale.

However, there are three key challenges companies need to address in orchestrating business growth in today's corporate environment: First, companies must understand the growth trajectories of their business. Rethinking the growth logic based on a strategic dialogue with customers is key to developing game-changer ideas for mutual growth. Second, companies must navigate the growth journey by executing jointly validated growth plans and continuously keeping the growth momentum. And third, companies must create favorable conditions for success through upskilling the right people to become orchestrators and growth champions, who play decisive roles in fostering that growth.

Addressing these challenges is why we've written *Triple Fit Strategy*. This book is based on twenty-five years of research and the in-depth observation of more than ten thousand business relationships on their quest to drive growth with their customers. The inception of Triple Fit Strategy began with Christoph's doctoral thesis generalizing his corporate-sales experience, resulting in the first conceptualization of the Triple Fit framework. After extensive field studies, the Triple Fit framework and its sub-concepts were further validated by Mehak in her doctoral thesis. Our work also led to the founding of Valuecreator AG, where we focus on guiding companies on their journey to build future-proof business relationships.

Our mission is to help you avoid costly breakdowns in business relationships and, instead, achieve breakthroughs by learning how to orchestrate growth. Building on a broad range of examples from different industries around the world, this book offers a diagnostic and action framework to create lasting customer relationships and boost growth. All tools and ideas have been successfully tested by us in business practice with large and small companies from Europe, the United States, and Asia.

The book is structured in three parts. In part I, we share the best practices of value creation across industries and geographies, leading to a completely different growth logic. No longer is it just about adding some growth of 5 or 10 percent here and there. Instead, it's about multiplying businesses and seeing relationships grow by two, three, or even ten times. Chapter 1 lays out Triple Fit Strategy at the highest level and introduces the core tool in your transformation: the Triple Fit canvas. Chapter 2 helps you identify and uncover the root causes of the specific challenges between your firm and a partner firm and begins to map a way forward in the near future as well as the long term. Chapters 2 and 3 also address the first steps to get started with a strategic customer dialogue and how to implement game-changer plans based on mutually agreed priorities.

In part II, we investigate how to walk the Triple Fit Strategy together with your customers at every level of the organization, from the boardroom to the front line. In chapter 4 we introduce how companies can evaluate the health of a particular portfolio of business relationships and allocate resources for breakthroughs. Chapter 5 takes a deep dive into the execution of validated growth plans and how to develop a three-year Triple Fit growth story. And in chapter 6, we will demonstrate tactics to overcome growth momentum killers and also introduce some supplementary tools to calibrate the growth journey further.

In part III, we lay out the steps to create favorable conditions for building lasting business relationships and boosting growth for the long term. The ultimate question to ask in all Triple Fit Strategy work is: "What if we were one company? How would we then work together?" Chapters 7 and 8 focus on the main protagonists that are involved in successfully orchestrating business relationships with customers. Chapter 7 shows how to master the transition from product selling to orchestrating value creation. In chapter 8, we shift the focus to the executive sponsors and the different roles they can (and should) assume when interacting with customers. And chapter 9 brings it all together by integrating Triple Fit principles and how to overcome implementation traps.

Triple Fit Strategy flips the product-centric view to a customer-centric view. Targeting three fit levels, you can orchestrate value creation based on a 360-degree perspective of customer priorities. The result will be customer-validated growth plans that do not only indicate breakthrough opportunities but are also a cross-check for your corporate strategy. We've seen time and again how understanding and implementing Triple Fit transforms businesses. This book gives you the knowledge and the tools to begin your growth journey. We encourage you to use the book as your guide to Triple Fit Strategy and to build lasting customer relationships and drive growth like never before.

Let's get to work.

PART I

UNDERSTANDING TRIPLE FIT TRAJECTORIES

CHAPTER 1

RETHINK THE
GROWTH LOGIC

It was a warm and pleasant early autumn day in Copenhagen, the vibrant Danish capital teeming with cyclists. At the heart of this contemporary, bustling city are the headquarters of shipping giant Maersk. And after months of preparation facilitated by us, a group of Maersk executives and account team members, had gathered in a conference room at HQ with counterparts from Kotahi Logistics, a joint venture between New Zealand's largest dairy food manufacturer Fonterra and largest meat exporter, Silver Fern Farms.[1]

Leading in the room were Moshe Loberant, Maersk's global key client director responsible for Kotahi, and Andrew Uasike, head of vendor management at Kotahi. Maersk's multiyear contract with Kotahi was coming up for renewal in less than twenty-four months. They were using this fact to figure out ways to expand the partnership and shape the next decade together, creating high growth for both companies. If they could get it right, the integrated supply chain between the two companies would help the New Zealand economy succeed on the global stage as Maersk took the shipping of Kotahi's customers' products global.

But to get it right, they'd need to unearth their common strategic issues and identify joint value-creation potential, which is why they were meeting in Copenhagen for the entire week. To ensure an ongoing successful collaboration, the right strategy was needed.

As long as business has existed, so has business strategy.[2] Defined as a set of guiding principles, strategy (or strategic moves) cascades into decision-making and resource allocation to overcome critical challenges and accomplish the desired objectives.[3] At least once or sometimes several times a year, top management teams at headquarters or leaders from regional teams in their respective offices enter the boardroom with lofty ambitions and the best of intentions, determined to assess their company situation with all its multifaceted problems and define the path forward toward a solution. After all, there's no point in going into a game without a game plan.

But this discussion between Maersk and Kotahi was different. It wasn't just a single company defining its strategy to beat the competition or redefine its product offerings for changing markets. It was two companies that were in a decade-long customer-supplier relationship, joining forces to define a common way forward and get there together. This is a bit more complicated than company strategy—after all, they needed a clear road map consisting of the guiding principles that would define the actions and priorities of *both* companies at once. But, as we'll find out, if they could get it right, the payoff would be exponential compared to a single-company strategy.

So what did Maersk and Kotahi do differently to create a jointly defined go-forward road map for their long-term business relationship? They applied what we call Triple Fit Strategy.

Triple Fit Strategy: A Blueprint for Mutual Growth

Triple Fit Strategy is all about putting customers at the heart of any business strategy and creating a fit at three levels: the planning fit, the execution fit, and the resources fit. Thus, the term "Triple Fit." Triple

FIGURE 1-1

Triple Fit Strategy in a business relationship

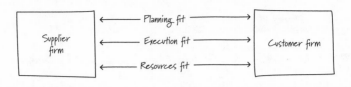

Fit Strategy consists of three guiding principles that make a jointly developed game-changing road map not only possible but a way of life for two companies in a strategic dialogue. Both companies must align their long-term vision and cocreate value with each other through the three levels of fit. The first principle focuses on the planning fit by re-aligning the plans to shift the strategy focus to customer priorities. The second principle focuses on the execution fit by reconfiguring it for the solutions design and their delivery. The third principle focuses on the resources fit by reallocating organizational assets for aligned growth (see figure 1-1).

Each of these three fits contains three building blocks that help you build your collaborative strategy. Let's take each in turn.

Planning fit: (Re-)aligning strategies with customer priorities

The planning fit comprises three building blocks—strategies, relationships, and communication—and indicates how closely a company's strategic direction is aligned with the customer's (see figure 1-2). In some cases, you can start with a simple alignment. In other cases, you want to realign strategies that may have gone offtrack. A supplier company must assess the degree to which its sales team takes the customer's strategy perspective into account and figure out how to use it to develop a joint three-year vision. The sales team must build and maintain multilevel contacts that promote stable relationships and communicate relevant information the customer needs for effective decision-making.

FIGURE 1-2

The planning fit in a business relationship

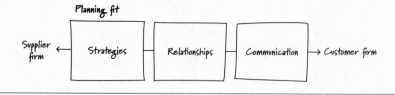

Execution fit: (Re-)configuring execution capabilities

The execution fit also comprises three building blocks—solutions, processes, and systems (see figure 1-3). This level shows how effectively suppliers execute the joint strategy by developing unique solutions and services that create value for customers, executing processes efficiently along the value chain, and implementing adequate systems for IT, financial, and legal support.

Resources fit: (Re-)allocating resources for mutual growth

The three building blocks in the resources fit are people, structures, and knowledge (see figure 1-4). This level indicates whether the supplier has the necessary resources to support customers, including trusted advisers with a customer-centric mindset, an adequately customer-centric organizational structure, and a dynamic learning environment for new-business generation.

FIGURE 1-3

The execution fit in a business relationship

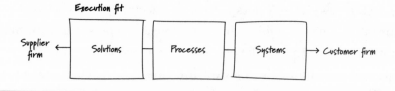

FIGURE 1-4

The resources fit in a business relationship

Resources fit
Supplier firm
People
Structures
Knowledge
Customer firm

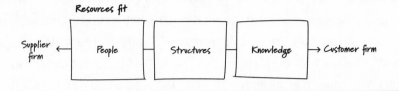

Triple Fit Canvas: A Diagnostic and Action Framework

Three fit levels with three buildings blocks each can be stacked together to provide a 360-degree perspective on a business relationship and its level of fit. For practical reasons, we have turned this view into the Triple Fit canvas, a visual tool that will serve as both a diagnostic and an action framework for business relationships (see figure 1-5). Our framework does not compete with other frameworks and canvases.[4] Instead, it extends the level of granularity through a more detailed level of analysis. In their seminal book *Blue Ocean Strategy*,

FIGURE 1-5

The Triple Fit canvas

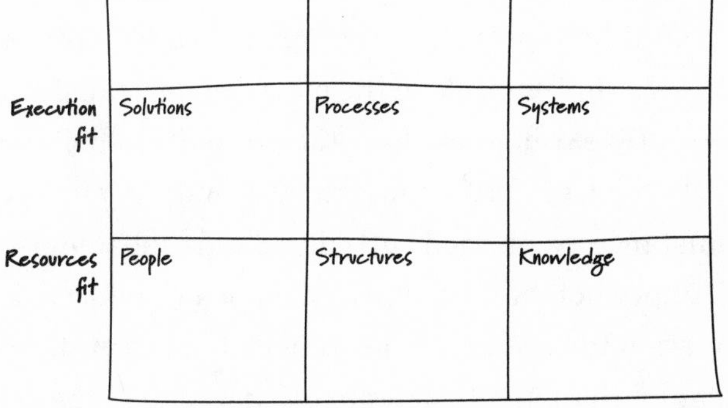

Planning fit
Strategies
Relationships
Communication
Execution fit
Solutions
Processes
Systems
Resources fit
People
Structures
Knowledge

for example, INSEAD professors W. Chan Kim and Renée Mauborgne address the creation of a new market space from a top-down perspective with the well-known Blue Ocean Strategy canvas. In contrast, the Triple Fit canvas addresses the relationship between companies from the bottom-up, playing field perspective. Similarly, the widely proliferated Business Model Canvas, developed by Alexander Osterwalder and Yves Pigneur, aims at generating viable business models for dedicated customer segments in different industries. In a complementing fashion, the Triple Fit canvas delivers insights and ideas for new business models or even a new blue ocean opportunity from a single business relationship perspective.

For any company that wants to orchestrate its customer relationships, the Triple Fit canvas is the starting point for a comprehensive analysis and pragmatic action planning. As strategies are formulated in different ways for different organizations, a good strategy diagnoses the underlying issues and leads to a solid action plan, and this is exactly what the Triple Fit canvas accomplishes between two firms. We mentioned before the value Kotahi saw in becoming a global player through its Maersk partnership. Maersk itself had much to gain as well. Using the Triple Fit canvas, Maersk's plan to transform its relationship with Kotahi can be summarized in nine ambition statements (see figure 1-6).

The Kotahi work was the tip of a massive strategic shift for a company that needed one. When Vincent Clerc took over as CEO of A. P. Moller-Maersk at the beginning of 2023, he knew he was in for a challenging mission. With the signs of a slowing economy after three years of record-high profits, the company had to completely rethink its growth logic and embark on the most radical transformation in its more than 100-year history that started in Svendborg, Denmark, in 1904. While the Covid-19 pandemic was ending, market and political circumstances remained turbulent, and global logistics demand was still unpredictable. In 2016, Maersk announced a significant transformation to become the leading global integrator of container logistics, more than just the company that had all the containers on the ocean, as many had thought of it. As former CEO of the ocean

FIGURE 1-6

Maersk's nine ambition statements for Kotahi

Planning fit	Strategies ① Focus on mutual strategic interests	Relationships ② Expand multilevel contact network	Communication ③ Establish a positive interaction
Execution fit	Solutions ④ Demonstrate unique ($) value of offerings	Processes ⑤ Coordinate activities across the value chain	Systems ⑥ Monitor and steer performance
Resources fit	People ⑦ Build the right skills and competencies	Structures ⑧ Align the organizational setup	Knowledge ⑨ Leverage expertise and assets

container division, Clerc took on the task of transitioning Maersk from simply moving ocean containers to providing end-to-end solutions, including inland logistics, port and terminal services, and supply chain expertise across different industries and geographies. The challenge was twofold: first, he had to keep the current level of ocean freight business as high as possible, while second, he needed to grow the share of newly added integrated transport and logistics services.

However, Maersk's sales efforts needed a new perspective at all levels to achieve this transformation. Still, too often, sales conversations centered around ocean container capacity and prices instead of looking into other areas of value to be created for—or even together with—the customer. Not surprisingly, customers were tempted to ask for a better price instead of appreciating Maersk's unique capabilities. Clerc knew that Maersk needed a customer-centric approach more than ever. It was critical to cater to customers' specific needs, ensuring that they had an appetite for the broader range of value propositions that Maersk offered. In order to do this, Maersk had to transition away from being still seen as the ocean container company and transform once and forever into a truly customer-centric company. So it turned to Triple Fit Strategy.

From Selling to Orchestrating Value

To achieve a customer-centric perspective, it is important to take a view beyond products and services, or what we represent in the Triple Fit canvas as the solutions building block. Because solutions provide just a limited inside-out view, you design and develop products based on internal logic in a limited value perspective without integrating the customer's view (see figure 1-7).

The other eight blocks help flip this to an outside-in view and, hence, multiply the touchpoints to create customer value many times. This shifts the focus from selling existing products and services to helping create new opportunities for mutual growth via a shared language that both parties can quickly learn to speak. Triple Fit Strategy invites the customer into a supplier's strategy formulation, execution, and resource-allocation decisions, as opposed to it being a passive bystander in the product-selling approach. Even though much has been written in research and practice about the importance of value creation, what remains missing was a hands-on approach to being able to achieve it in the real world.[5]

FIGURE 1-7

Product-centric (inside-out) versus customer-centric (outside-in) perspective

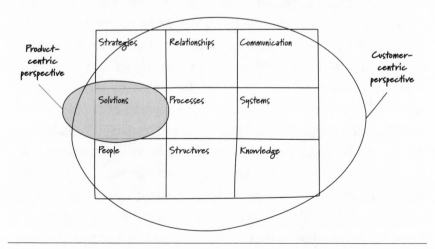

As we stated in the introduction, the ultimate question to ask in all Triple Fit discussions is: "What if we were one company? How would we then work together?" And this was exactly the question that drove the discussion between Maersk and Kotahi to a new level.

Given our experience with best practices in value creation across industries and geographies, we were able to observe value creation leading to a completely different growth logic that created financial impact. Consider, for example, Evonik Industries, a German specialty-chemicals group, that used an early version of the Triple Fit canvas to integrate customer perspectives into its product development. That large-scale project focused on creating proactive, strategic value for Evonik's three hundred biggest customers. Six months after conducting the initial conversations, Evonik signed a deal worth €150 million with one of its largest automotive customers. The company attributed the contract to the Triple Fit discussion. Evonik also believes that the process helped it weather industry downturns better than its competitors. Evonik still uses the Triple Fit approach to orchestrate customer relationships, such as with a US-based food company which added €40 million in new business, while Evonik scored €10 million in new business, thanks to a joint Triple Fit effort.

Why Triple Fit Works

The reason Triple Fit creates results is because it allows the constituents to address the following three key challenges:

1. Overcome the product-centric mindset

2. Escape the buyer-seller trap

3. Build a customer-centric organization

Let's look at each in more detail.

Challenge 1: Overcome the
product-centric mindset

The dialogue with Kotahi exposed a general sense among its customers Maersk had not known about. Increasingly, Maersk's customers had questioned the supplier's top-down directional approach. The structured Triple Fit dialogue started to redirect Maersk to an area that became a higher priority than before: customer-centricity. Maersk began realizing the need to become customer-led as against the shipping industry's product-focused tradition.

For any company with a strong tradition of leading innovation through superior product development, it faces the risk of a product-centric mindset. Consider, for example, companies in the machine-tooling industry in Germany and Switzerland, where systems with impressive scientific and technological features hit the markets, but customers don't always have an appetite for buying them.[6] Not surprisingly, many of these companies either closed shop or were sold to more commercially oriented competitors or investors. From our own experience in corporate life and research across industries, we can confirm that the internal motto of many of these product-focused companies can be characterized as: "We have Swiss precision and German engineering, but stupid customers."

This is exactly what a product-centric mindset is—a strategy to build newer and more advanced products regardless of market demand. Coupled with a misconstrued sense of pride in their products and a somewhat falsely arrogant belief that their products' superiority will create a market can be a very dangerous position.[7] Because, in the end, the market is a true mirror of real customer demands. As for the fate of many unsuccessful product-centric companies, the customer always wins and is always right, leading to a sales growth that never comes.[8] Prominent examples include Xerox, focusing on high-end printing and copying machines while neglecting the demand from small businesses for more affordable, smaller machines; or IBM, keeping the focus on mainframe computers instead of participating in the growing personal computer market that took over the business world in record time.[9]

The reason it is hard to be customer-centric, especially in a business-to-business (B2B) market, is because it requires a shift from a product-centric mindset that companies often fall into. The product-centric mindset is based on establishing a product-market fit with their customers. The underlying hypothesis is that the stronger your product-market fit is, the bigger the mutually beneficial outcomes.[10]

The product-market fit is not a customer-centric approach because it only focuses on an isolated part in the business relationship, and it excludes mutually beneficial outcomes. By definition, a product-market fit is designed to maximize the seller outcome.[11] Indeed, many organizations struggle to exploit mutually beneficial outcomes. The reasons for these struggles are manifold, but our research shows there are just two main reasons:

- One or both sides are not looking at the big picture but are focused on the old-fashioned volume-price negotiation, causing relationship breakdowns.

- The efforts to achieve mutual benefits are not aligned due to conflicting priorities, hindering the move from breakdowns to breakthroughs.

That's what one of our clients, a supplier of industrial process automation solutions we call Checkmate to protect its identity, experienced. Eager to create a lasting impression in its markets, Checkmate distributed a high-end, expensive-to-produce brochure pointing out the many applications the company could serve with its high-quality solutions. The crucial part of the brochure said this: "We define a strategic business relationship between our customers and Checkmate as a long-term commitment dedicated to lowering costs and increasing revenues for both companies." To the surprise of Checkmate, customer feedback was not as positive as expected. Customers weren't buying its customer-centricity. One customer said: "You could be doing five times the business with us if you got your act together. You work with most of our organization but focus on nothing of relevance to us!"[12]

What a quote! On the one hand, it pointed out the future business potential Checkmate had. But on the other hand, it addressed a hidden flaw in the supplier's approach. While the brochure was printed with all the best intentions, and the promise of mutual benefits sounded appealing, the supplier did not walk the talk. Checkmate did not change its product-centric view and still applied old-school, inside-out sales tactics.

So, while the idea of the product-market fit has appeal, it also has clear limitations. For many companies in the business-to-business domain, the product-market fit stands and falls with the correct identification and targeting of the right customers whose needs best fit what they have, their existing products and services.[13] They then develop a polished value proposition, which they communicate aggressively to the market. The focus is solely on what a company's products can do for the customer and make the transaction. Missing from this approach is what Checkmate promised but didn't deliver: how two parties can create value together. This is a classic dead end on an organization's path to customer-centricity. And the question about how much value could be created beyond the notorious product-market fit and what would happen if the perspective on selling value were expanded to creating value remains to be answered.

Our work with leading global companies needing help to create growth despite their best strategic expertise made us realize that this struggle results from a too-narrow point of view. We found that the traditional strategic perspective in B2B sales was still centered around seeing business customers as a movie audience. The supplier companies were like the production houses, where creating the movie was their process and the movie itself was their product. Put it out there and see who buys it. This led to the most important business customers being involved only in customer feedback or customer satisfaction survey stages ("Did you like the movie?"), with the supplier companies fervently hoping that their movie would create a breakthrough at the box office and that the audience would love it. If that didn't happen, strategic thinking at best was guiding them to create new kinds of movies (new products) or find a new audience (new markets) that would appreciate their existing products.[14]

What we saw, though, was that the companies that were *not* struggling to create growth were not making movies in isolation. They were doing it differently. Their business customers were hardly just an audience; they were an integral part of the movie production process, from script writing, budget planning, production scheduling, and casting of the lead roles to directing and delivering the film. An impeccable collaboration was in place, and many different building blocks were in play in this journey. And why shouldn't they be? After all, the business customers are the firms, not the individuals, so they have the resources and strategies to create tangible outcomes. They have the know-how on the industry, markets, and products, including the awareness of emerging technologies and innovation megatrends. They have the best view of competitors, especially if they are part of their share of wallet for the overall revenue. They know the gaps in business models and operational effectiveness of their supplier firm. And finally, they want to unlock growth just as much as their supplier does. But to unlock growth, companies must be able and willing to meet one precondition, and that is to escape the proverbial buyer-seller trap.

Challenge 2: Escape the buyer-seller trap

If the only way to foster lasting business relationships and create customer breakthroughs is to expand the limited, product-centric view to a fully customer-centric perspective, then what was stopping Maersk, or any company, from achieving this? In our research, we have found that only 15 percent of sellers (and buyers) adopt and practice a broader perspective on value creation. According to our data, 85 percent of the protagonists in business-to-business conversations are stuck in the proverbial buyer-seller trap, where discussions between the two parties are focused primarily on the transaction, specifically, cost-cutting and price reductions.[15]

But often, these discussions are fundamentally adversarial. You are set up for relationship breakdowns when the goal is to beat each other up in the annual cost negotiations and price bargaining and *win* the transaction. Consider the retail industry, where international buying group AgeCore confronted Nestlé with a breakdown and delisting of 150 items due to unmet price-cutting requests, a confrontation similar to others with manufacturers AB InBev, Mars, PepsiCo, and Coca-Cola.[16] Or look at the automotive industry, where higher raw material prices and just-in-time inventory have increased tensions throughout the B2B supply chain. A prominent example is the long dispute between Volkswagen and its parts supplier Prevent, a case that led to a complete breakdown of the twenty-five-year business relationship. Over several years, both parties accused each other of unlawfully stopping supply of price increases on seat covers and brake discs and sued each other for hundreds of millions in damages.[17]

And, in our practical work with companies around the globe, we see the same trend to adopt the hard-core, low-level purchasing behavior of the retail and automotive industries in other industries, such as pharmaceuticals. Coupled with the growing demands to control the costs of goods and the increasingly complex skein of global regulations, these developments pose a real threat to the innovation efforts of many pharmaceutical companies. On the other hand, if prices are not controlled, only rich countries may be able to pay for high-performance drugs, which in turn causes a whole set of new implications. As an outside observer, one can sometimes only wonder why companies do not behave differently, as all these disputes in the buyer-seller trap destroy so much value for no result.

Rather than focus on how much value such conflicts destroy, we focus on the more interesting question of how much value will be created if such disputes could be solved or avoided? Isn't there a better way than falling back to (or remaining in) a transactional mode and confronting business partners with an impossible threat to win at least something in the end? What if there were a new way of looking at the situation, leading to more relationship breakthroughs instead of breakdowns? What if a company could escape the buyer-seller trap and become the most customer-centric company in its industry? This is exactly what Triple Fit helps companies do.

For Maersk, the growth breakthrough came with overcoming these very challenges, which started with the weeklong meeting with Kotahi in Copenhagen. In the presence of both CEOs, David Ross from Kotahi and Vincent Clerc from Maersk, the joint team pitched a one-page Triple Fit Strategy road map with a three-year plan to take Kotahi's customers' products from New Zealand to the world more effectively and more efficiently. The Triple Fit Strategy approach revealed a potential total value of short-term additional business opportunities for both companies, unlocking a value of several hundred million dollars. Eighteen months later, the next long-term contract was signed, resulting in a robust shipping network to deliver products worth a business volume of billions of dollars from New Zealand around the globe.

Given the radical success of this case and a few other pilot cases we will see later in the book, Maersk pivoted to a new ambition: to apply Triple Fit to redefine customer-centricity for all its strategic customers. Triple Fit Strategy has changed the way Maersk approaches customers, and the way it aligns itself internally, serving as an exemplary success story or what we call a lighthouse case for other global companies on the same path, creating a cascading effect of Triple Fit success cases and breakthrough growth stories that continue to surprise, delight, and humble us with the power of a simple strategic tool. But there is a third challenge that stands in the way.

Challenge 3: Build a customer-centric organization

Every company is constantly navigating change and working to get its strategy right, almost as if answering a call to the motto "disrupt or be disrupted." Leaders dream of coming up with a strategy that delivers innovative solutions that trounce the competition (until new competition comes along), or that leads to creative breakthroughs that have the power to transform humanity—even save lives. And if they can get there, the reward is the pot of gold—the revenue and profit to survive in hard times and thrive in good times, year after year.

However, amid all difficult economic circumstances and unpredictable political situations, what sometimes gets forgotten is the essence of why a company even matters to the world in the first place.[18] It matters because of its customers. If there are no customers, no company will stay in business for long. That being customer-centric is important is an understatement; it is the heart of why business exists. Thus, getting strategy right is about making customers central to any business strategy.[19]

We define customer-centricity as follows: orchestrating all company activities for its target customers' success at a profit. Therefore, customer-centricity demands that companies remain in constant conversation with their customers, identify strategic insights that emerge from the dialogue, and act on them to navigate change and transform how they do business. In the end, customer-centricity is about working together, delivering jointly developed solutions that create mutually beneficial outcomes for both the supplier and the customer. That means strategy requires you to look to your customer, not just to your competitors and the market, to set your strategic direction.[20]

The biggest barrier to getting customer-centricity right is conflating it with *consumer*-centricity. The latter involves customer satisfaction surveys, net promotor score tracking, mapping customer journeys, keeping the customers engaged via a responsive website, using chatbots and AI solutions, and so on.[21] Highly valued consumer-centric brands like Apple, Google, and Amazon do exactly this. They deliver more value than their customers expect.[22]

But what does customer-centricity look like when you are in the business-to-business domain? What if you were like Maersk competing in the shipping industry and your customers are other organizations like Kotahi, not individual consumers? How do you achieve an impressive year-on-year, profitable growth with your customers, while aligning your strategies, value propositions, supply chain processes, and resources?

This will be our focus, the business-to-business arena, because customer-centricity is both different and less well understood there, despite the fact it's the bigger market. Behind the scenes of the glamorous business-to-consumer (B2C) market is the global B2B market, valued at $14.9 trillion (about four times the size of B2C) and accounting for almost 80 percent of the global daily transactions.[23] All told, there is a ten times bigger profit pool if you also look to B2B and develop customer-centricity there.[24]

Even the retail-customer-focusing tech giants Apple, Google. and Amazon make billions of dollars in their business partnerships with high-tech companies through software and services deals. Consider, for example, Amazon's collaboration since 2022 with Italy-based automaker Stellantis to deliver software by 2024 for millions of Stellantis vehicles globally, including brands like Jeep, Chrysler, Fiat, Ram, and Peugeot. This partnership to codevelop the software platform, which leverages AI and cloud solutions to create personalized, intuitive in-vehicle experiences for entertainment, Alexa-enabled voice assistance, navigation, vehicle maintenance, e-commerce marketplaces, and payment services, is a part of the Stellantis's ambition to invest more than $33.7 billion through 2025 into software and electrification. It is helping both companies move forward into business breakthroughs.[25] More examples of Amazon's partnerships in the government context are its $600 million deal with the CIA in 2013, followed by a new "AWS Secret Region" for the US intelligence community and US government customers in 2017, and a $10 billion cloud computing contract with the US National Security Agency after a very public lawsuit dispute with competitor Microsoft in 2021–2022, all of which showcases the importance of B2B partnerships for these large tech companies.[26]

In B2B, customer-centricity is more than customer satisfaction surveys and so forth. At a basic level, it usually starts with negotiating and renegotiating contracts, designing tailored value propositions, developing cutting-edge digital sales journeys, making sales-growth predictions through the latest data-driven analytics, and mitigating the endless risks that come with two or more organizations dealing with each other.

At an advanced level, customer-centricity for business customers means having a business strategy that incorporates the customer's voice. Our research shows that B2B companies aspiring to be customer-centric ensure that the voice of their business customers is represented in the boardroom when business strategies are formulated.[27] This saves them from the classic risk of making strategy discussions the equivalent of a ritual rain dance: it has no effect on the weather that follows, but it makes those who engage in it feel that they are in control.[28]

Business customers are the most important source of information about the market (and thus, information that informs strategy), as they provide firsthand insights not only on industry developments and innovations, but also on shaping commercial innovation trends through their own strategies that will influence the future decisions in their business with the supplier firm. For any business strategy to overlook business customer insights and information is an expensive risk, especially for the large customers that contribute a significant part of the company's revenue. A case in point is Microsoft and its ill-fated Nokia acquisition. At the time of the decision to enter the device market, many of Microsoft's customers were not convinced that this was the right strategic move.[29] However, the management went forward with the acquisition that was seven years later pulled out of devices business with Nokia. The Microsoft management would have seen it coming if they had listened to the strategy inputs of their key accounts. Since then, a lot has changed, and the company has become much more customer-centric under the leadership of Satya Nadella.[30]

When Maersk first began a strategic dialogue with its business customer Kotahi, it realized that there was not enough alignment between the top management teams. Also, the sharing of strategic plans was missing, including a mutual go-forward strategy across the supply chain network for ocean transport, ports, and landside logistics. In some cases, the missing communication was blocking the customer's approval of new value proposition proposals from Maersk. As a result, there were few joint activities to broaden the relationship. What was needed was a customer-centric approach, because Kotahi was an important customer for Maersk. Making the voice of the customer heard in the boardroom was key for further success. The meetings in Copenhagen showed the companies that there was massive value just sitting there, if they could talk and unlock it together.

So let's find out how to implement it.

TAKEAWAYS

- Triple Fit Strategy is all about putting customers at the heart of any business strategy and going beyond the product-market fit to create a robust road map for mutual growth.

- The Triple Fit canvas consists of three fit levels, planning, execution, and resources, which make a jointly developed game-changing road map possible through a strategic dialogue.

- Triple Fit Strategy works because it helps companies overcome the product-centric mindset, escape the buyer-seller trap, and build a customer-centric organization.

REFLECTION QUESTIONS

- What is your company's dominant perspective about business relationships: Is it product-centric or customer-centric?

- What are the Triple Fit Strategy ambitions for your industry? Use the blank canvas in this chapter (figure 1-5) or download a free canvas from triplefitstrategy.com to fill in.

- Which of your business relationships could benefit from a strategic dialogue based on the Triple Fit canvas? Keep these relationships in mind for subsequent chapters.

CHAPTER 2

INITIATE A STRATEGIC DIALOGUE

The summer of 2007 was an exciting time for the Sonos team. Sonos, a fast-growing manufacturer of luxury wireless-audio systems, struck a deal with the US-based retailer Best Buy to sell its products at more than six hundred retail locations across the United States.[1] Both sides touted it as the proverbial win-win. Sonos would be spotlighted in Best Buy stores with live, interactive demonstrations. In return, Best Buy would gain access to the best-reviewed new audio systems in the world. But ten years later, profit margins for both companies were eroding; tensions ran high as Sonos increasingly surprised Best Buy with short notice information such as last-minute promotion changes. Best Buy perceived a lack of strategic alignment; Sonos was worried about the departures of key Best Buy personnel who had championed the partnership.

In 2018, when we facilitated a Triple Fit workshop for Sonos at Best Buy's Minneapolis headquarters, a Best Buy executive gave the Sonos team an ultimatum: come up with better terms for the partnership or there was no good reason to continue the meeting. The two companies framed the conversation in that meeting using the Triple Fit canvas that we introduced in chapter 1. It prompted the members of their teams to ask and answer questions such as: What are our combined strengths and weaknesses? What does the other party think of us? What can we do to improve the relationship? As sometimes happens with good Triple Fit discussions, it grew heated. The teams were brutally critical of each other. Halfway through, the Best Buy executive expressed his growing frustration. "What is the point of this exercise?" he asked. "We only need a few actions to improve our margins; otherwise, we shouldn't waste each other's time."

But people from both sides, many of whom had sat silently during the blunt back-and-forth, argued in support of continuing the exercise. After years of narrow discussions focused on tactics and pricing, it was the first time the two teams had openly spoken about larger issues of strategy and collaboration. Criticism was better than silence, they reasoned. At one point, a Best Buy supply chain executive argued that two recommendations Sonos had made—increase process efficiency and communicate more frequently—would have a greater positive impact on Best Buy than a discount would. So, despite the original ultimatum, the Best Buy team agreed to continue the meeting without an offer from Sonos to cut prices any further.

Even though it was scheduled for only the morning, the meeting ran the whole working day. Both teams laid options on the table and agreed on breakthrough ideas. At the end of the day, both teams walked out with a jointly developed strategy road map based on the motto "Aligning for further growth as if we were one firm." One year later, both teams attributed improved business alignment and above-average growth rates to the Triple Fit exercise and the resulting strategy shift.

How Triple Fit Works

What exactly unfolded in the meeting that led two previously warring parties to join forces? What made the seemingly adversarial teams find common ground for collaborating on their most strategic issues and addressing them head-on, maybe for the first time? What made a

FIGURE 2-1

The sequence of the Triple Fit process

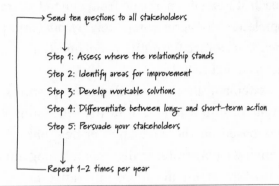

→ Send ten questions to all stakeholders

Step 1: Assess where the relationship stands
Step 2: Identify areas for improvement
Step 3: Develop workable solutions
Step 4: Differentiate between long- and short-term action
Step 5: Persuade your stakeholders

Repeat 1-2 times per year

jointly developed road map possible, as if these companies were one? It was the strategic dialogue with each other based on a five-step process completed in a one-day workshop (see figure 2-1).

The best sales teams we have worked with have helped their clients create value through new initiatives they created by having a deep discussion about what they can do together—not by fitting existing products into an existing strategy.[2] High-performing business relationships start with a broader conversation about how both parties can shape the future together—the strategic dialogue.[3]

The clear focus on a strategic dialogue instead of on the product-market fit also led Sonos and Best Buy to a fresh value-creation focus that shifted their business relationship radically. Let's have a look at each process step in more detail.

Step 1: Assess where the relationship stands

The Triple Fit canvas consists of nine building blocks representing critical areas to build a long-term strategic relationship that fosters sustainable growth. Strategic dialogue begins with understanding where both companies see each other on these critical parameters. The tool we propose for doing this is a questionnaire we call the "relationship maturity check"—a series of ten statements that focus on how well you collaborate with each other. To get started, rate the accuracy of each statement on a scale from one to five (ranging from "disagree completely" to "agree completely") *from the perspective of a given customer.* You can see the entire list of questions mapped to the Triple Fit canvas in figure 2-2.

The first statement in the questionnaire captures an overall view of the relationship, while each of the other nine represents a building block based on the company's critical objectives with its customers, ranging from strategic alignment, strong multilevel relationships, consistent communication, innovative products, aligned processes and systems, value-creation-focused people, to supportive

FIGURE 2-2

How close are you to your customer?

Use the ten statements below to rate your company from your customer's perspective, with 1 equaling "disagree completely" and 5 equaling "agree completely." To achieve an accentuated picture, we recommend entering only full ratings, i.e., 1, 2, or 3, etc., and not half-ratings like 1.5, or 2.3, or similar.

Overall, we rate our relationship with [Supplier] as. . .   ☐1 ☐2 ☐3 ☐4 ☐5

Planning fit	Strategies	Relationships	Communication
	[Supplier] uses a mutually agreed-upon collaboration strategy with us	[Supplier] maintains strong contacts with us from the operational to the executive level	[Supplier] communicates in an open, fair, and forward-looking way with us
	☐1 ☐2 ☐3 ☐4 ☐5	☐1 ☐2 ☐3 ☐4 ☐5	☐1 ☐2 ☐3 ☐4 ☐5
Execution fit	Solutions	Processes	Systems
	[Supplier] develops unique offerings and value propositions for us	[Supplier] aligns processes effectively and efficiently along our value chain	[Supplier] does business with us using compatible IT, finance and legal systems
	☐1 ☐2 ☐3 ☐4 ☐5	☐1 ☐2 ☐3 ☐4 ☐5	☐1 ☐2 ☐3 ☐4 ☐5
Resources fit	People	Structures	Knowledge
	[Supplier] assigns people with the ability to act as trusted advisers to us	[Supplier] provides cross-functional organizational and support structures for us	[Supplier] uses its knowledge to cocreate more profitable business with us
	☐1 ☐2 ☐3 ☐4 ☐5	☐1 ☐2 ☐3 ☐4 ☐5	☐1 ☐2 ☐3 ☐4 ☐5

organizational structures and resources. The questionnaire helps detect the current state of knowledge, learning, and skills shared between the organizations and identify the gaps to address to foster innovation and build the right strategic capabilities and efficiencies that will deliver higher value for both companies.

To overcome self-reporting bias, this step must ideally be accomplished with the *customer* rating the accuracy of each statement as well. This can be done by sending the questionnaire to multiple contacts in different departments, verticals, regions, and so on on the customer side to get a wide picture about the perceived relationship from different perspectives. If you give your team high ratings and your customer agrees, you probably have a solid, prosperous relationship. Low ratings, obviously, signify that your relationship needs improvement. To achieve a high-performing relationship, you should aspire to as many fives as possible, which is exactly what the other four steps in the Triple Fit process help to accomplish. But at this step, an honest, unbiased assessment, even if it means a low rating, is the make-or-break deal.

While it is appealing to think that a world-class strategic dialogue arises from clever thinking, capturing every minute detail of the issue at hand, more often than not, it grows out of experience based on a big-picture perspective of the situation.[4] The strength of this dialogue is not based on complicated and detailed predictions of the future but on understanding the existing situation beyond tactical behavior represented by unreasonably low ratings. An often-observed example is high ratings except for "solutions" motivated by a tactical focus on getting a price discount. Another frequent example is higher customer ratings and lower supplier ratings. There are two options to deal with high customer ratings: either you thank the customer for its generous rating and go back to daily business, or you use your more critical view of some Triple Fit building blocks to instruct the customer about some flaws in the relationship it hasn't been aware of, and agree on corrective actions that create value for the customer.

The latter approach may push some old-school sellers out of their comfort zone. But sharing your findings openly with customers can lead to rewarding outcomes.[5] In 2021, Virginie Jackson, a key account manager at DSM, took the company's Triple Fit self-assessment to one customer, a producer of dairy products, for feedback. The customer offered to discuss collaboration hurdles and areas where value creation would be of mutual interest. After those discussions, the two parties agreed to reduce the number of unprofitable SKUs on offer. This action was primarily beneficial for the customer, as it killed some existing sales for DSM. But the proposed move created a great deal of trust and appetite for further ideas. Next, a joint value-creation team initiated co-development and sustainability projects to support the customer's mission to become an all-natural organic-product leader. As a result of that meeting and subsequent conversations, DSM doubled the value of the dairy producer's pilot program, while also improving its own revenue by nearly €1 million in less than a year.

This is why we recommend starting a strategic dialogue with the ten-statement template in the questionnaire. After the results are in, it's all about going deep in the discussion to find out the real motivation behind each rating based on a 360-degree perspective. By deliberately asking only a few questions, the questionnaire gives companies using it the following four immediate benefits:

- It creates a snapshot that can be repeated over time, usually every six to twelve months.

- It flags the strengths and weaknesses of a business relationship via the rating scale.

- It is easily understood by stakeholders at all levels, creating high engagement.

- It is fast to fill in since it doesn't take more than ten to fifteen minutes to complete.

When Sonos sent the questionnaire to its customer Best Buy, it helped both companies identify their strengths and weaknesses in an easy-to-understand way. Having the aggregate rating numbers from both these companies displayed next to each other sparked a strategic dialogue when the companies met. While Best Buy appreciated Sonos for creating products that provided a great experience and had a strong brand positioning and loved its willingness to pilot or partner new initiatives, it also found that the key performance indicators (KPIs) of the two companies were not aligned, and it didn't like that Sonos was also driving its own direct sales, which competed with Best Buy. For its part, Sonos appreciated Best Buy for its dedicated field teams helping create some of the best in-store displays in the industry and its subject-matter experts who helped focus on collaborative solutions. On top of that, there were some communication challenges and minimal relationships at the senior executive level, and critical decisions were often made without any input, leading to missed opportunities and inconsistent mutual goals. Figure 2-3 gives the initial customer ratings at the start of the workshop.

FIGURE 2-3

How Best Buy rated Sonos at the start of the Triple Fit workshop

	Overall, we rate our relationship with Sonos as. . . 1 2 **3** 4 5		
Planning fit	Strategies — Sonos uses a mutually agreed upon collaboration strategy with us — 1 2 3 4 5	Relationships — Sonos maintains strong contacts with us from the operational to the executive level — 1 2 3 4 5	Communication — Sonos communicates in an open, fair, and forward-looking way with us — 1 2 **3** 4 5
Execution fit	Solutions — Sonos develops unique offerings and value propositions for us — 1 2 **3** 4 5	Processes — Sonos aligns processes effectively and efficiently along our value chain — 1 **2** 3 4 5	Systems — Sonos does business with us using compatible IT, finance, and legal systems — 1 2 3 4 5
Resources fit	People — Sonos assigns people with the ability to act as trusted advisers to us — 1 2 3 **4** 5	Structures — Sonos provides cross-functional organizational and support structures for us — 1 2 3 **4** 5	Knowledge — Sonos uses its knowledge to cocreate more profitable business with us — 1 2 **3** 4 5

It often surprises us how quickly the conversation between two companies takes off after this simple exercise. It seems to open the floodgates for further dialogue because, for the first time, the companies are able to understand each other's perspective on critical building blocks to the relationship and are able to notice patterns in their communication and behavior. More than once we have heard customers say to the supplier firm after the first Triple Fit process step: "This is the first time ever that we discussed beneficial improvements for us instead of you trying to sell us something!" No further comments needed.

Step 2: Identify areas for improvement

After you've completed the relationship assessment, you must identify why you succeed or struggle in particular areas. A proven approach is to let the team ask why the ratings are the way they are. Why do you succeed or struggle in particular areas? Asking why you are in this position can help clarify the strengths that led to a high rating or the weaknesses that prevented one. In areas where you received unsatisfactory scores, ask "Why?" up to five times, until the root cause is properly defined, enlisting your customer's help in answering. If you feel more comfortable using other techniques—for example, fishbone diagrams—that's also fine. The ambition is to get to the root cause that explains a certain rating better than just a symptom observation.[6]

Asking why several times is based on the Toyota principle that helps different parties identify the core issues and leads them to the heart of the obstacle that is preventing the growth or strategic turnaround.[7] The company and its customer often represent two different perspectives with completely different industries and market focus, and hence, the identification of critical strengths and weaknesses involves understanding why certain areas are rated lower than others so that these perspectives can be brought into light and shared in an honest conversation. Having an outside-in perspective means that companies can look for patterns that help them get closer to the core of explaining their strengths and weaknesses, and this is exactly what this step aims to accomplish.

To improve its relationship with a major bank, Vodafone's sales team, led by Keith Shaw, then the Vodafone global account manager, performed a Triple Fit analysis in 2018. It focused on obvious value deficits between the two companies and the financial and operational risk associated with aligning their values. Teams from the two companies realized that the customer needed to prepare its technology for the future of mobile banking. With a game plan developed using the Triple Fit analysis, the two partnered to map the technology consumption of tens of thousands of the bank's employees—information they used to develop the technical requirements for a new "bring your own device" policy at the bank. Driven by Covid-19, a draft working-from-home policy had to be accelerated, which led to the deployment of new advanced remote-communication solutions. Meetings for top executives from both companies were consistently held to maintain collaborative momentum. They included regular status checks, during which the Triple Fit canvas was used to initiate new value creation. Vodafone's business with the bank increased by 11 percent annually over the next three years, and its opportunity pipeline increased by 30 percent.

To complete this step, you may want to reconsider your ratings and, if necessary, adjust them. The following four questions help to cross-check the discussion content:

- What are the reasons for the ratings (and their gaps)?

- What strength(s) got us to the current score and why?

- What weakness(es) prevented a five-star rating and why?

- What are the associated risks and their potential impact?

When Sonos and Best Buy got to this conversation step, they realized that there were several mutual strengths in place because the ratings had confirmed a good overall perception of relationship

FIGURE 2-4

Mutually agreed-upon strategic priorities during the Sonos–Best Buy workshop

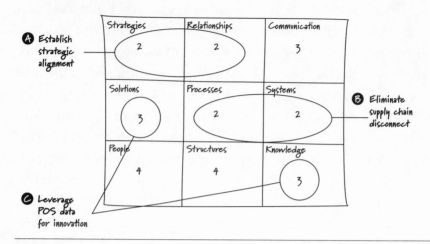

performance. However, to take the relationship from good to great, they needed to work on the lower-rated areas, such as not having joint promotion planning, communication out of sync, and a lack of executive-level communication that led to short-notice crises. At the same time, they could build on the areas in which they were already aligned with high scores from each side. In essence, the two teams agreed on three strategic priorities (see figure 2-4).

Step 3: Develop workable solutions

The results of step two are the basis for developing ideas to boost value and mitigate risk. Asking what needs to be done to improve (or maintain) the situation is a simple but powerful way of looking at your full range of options. Don't jump to conclusions (or actions) too quickly. Most salespeople with a product-centric mindset tend to skip this step and then wonder why their solutions failed. A superior approach maps the spectrum of reasonable options, prioritizes and selects the most promising ideas, and secures the support of everyone who must be involved.

The Schindler Group, a Switzerland-based manufacturer of escalators, walkways, and elevators, had been in contact with a multinational construction, property, and infrastructure company for several years. In 2019 Michael Dobler, Schindler's senior vice president of global key accounts, proposed using the Triple Fit process to codevelop new business. The infrastructure company was intrigued: it had never discussed business issues with a supplier, beyond product and price configurations. The conversations led to cost-saving initiatives and increased product quality and safety levels. Triple Fit helped the infrastructure company save more than $16 million over a two-year period. The customer awarded Schindler a large portion of its business and full visibility into its project pipeline for the next ten years. Schindler still uses the Triple Fit canvas to evaluate potential relationships and to draw a strategy road map for joint value creation with existing customers. "The Triple Fit canvas helps us develop high-value relationships with customers and project partners and run them like a business," Dobler says.[8]

To continue the strategic dialogue at this stage, focus on the most important building blocks first. Ask, "What needs to be done now?" and jointly develop a range of ideas to address the identified deficits and shortcomings. Ensure that the ideas create value and mitigate risks for *both* parties. Use the following four questions for a cross-check of contents:

- What common objectives would drive mutual value creation?

- What needs to be done to create value?

- What needs to be done to mitigate risks?

- What needs to be done to foster a lasting relationship?

The actions the companies define at this stage are not based on a one-size-fits-all approach or done as a onetime year-end strategy review where the companies define their next actions from a high level but are based on real-time challenges and existing situations that need attention. This is exactly what the Triple Fit process aims to identify: workable ideas that both the companies can take to address their performance gaps.

For example, when Sonos entered this dialogue step with Best Buy and asked, "What needs to be done now?" the companies decided that they needed a joint Best Buy–Sonos team to orchestrate cross-functional efforts and eliminate challenges resulting from the identified supply chain disconnect. Further, they proposed executive sponsors to help clear internal hurdles, when necessary, thus bridging the gap for missing executive-level relationships and combining solutions and knowledge for aligning on the delivery timings and ensuring well-customized marketing solutions. The heart of what made the strategic dialogue at this step a success was deciding to find outcomes where they both acted, effectively, as one company. These simple steps opened doors for many new initiatives and innovations that would drive growth for both the companies.

Step 4: Differentiate between long- and short-term actions

This step of the strategic dialogue brings teams from the planning to execution. While it is important to identify critical next actions in general, what makes them a reality in the daily business is establishing long-term and short-term timelines to execute the same. To complete this step, you first want to revisit your ideas on value creation and risk mitigation. Try to describe specific actions as concretely as possible (Who does what, until when, and how?). Then, split your activities into two categories: ninety-day quick-win actions and long-term projects with a timeline of up to three years. Enter estimated costs and projected return (robust assumptions are sufficient). Validate the proposed actions and projects with your counterpart. To garner stakeholder support, use the motto "Show me the money!" to describe exactly how each action will be executed and deliver value.

Konica Minolta applied this approach to its relationship with the BMW Group. Konica's business solutions division had recently started deploying multifunctional devices, printers, and plotters for BMW. Both parties soon recognized that BMW's intense focus on price and hardware was hindering value creation. The Konica team ran a Triple Fit analysis with BMW to see where it could improve. The collaboration led to multiple immediate innovations—among them enabling BMW employees to print documents and images from any device and import scanned data to mobile devices—along with several large-scale, longer-term improvements in mobile-device workflow productivity. As a result, BMW saved money and improved processes at its global production centers. Both companies agreed on a long-term partnership that increased the size of the BMW account for Konica by 300 percent.

To cross-check what you come up with, answer the following four questions:

- Did you clarify per action and project who is doing what until when?

- Did you specify the required decisions to take per action and project by both parties?

- What is the estimated investment (money, time, etc.)?

- What is the potential return (money, other)?

For Sonos and Best Buy, this was a truly groundbreaking step of the conversation. As shown in figure 2-4, they defined and mapped three initiatives. The first focused on establishing a strategic dialogue by scheduling the first top-to-top meeting in the next quarter. The second initiative focused on eliminating the disconnects by identifying global supply chain and logistics partners. And the third focused on leveraging data for innovation by integrating their learnings in joint product and display planning. The concrete actions in each of these initiatives were further defined in terms of the time and financial investment required and the stakeholders who would be involved. This gave both the companies a clear go-forward road map for both the short and long terms.

To sum up the first four steps of the Triple Fit process, we start with assessing the relationship performance (step 1), then diving deeper with the questions of why (step 2), what (step 3), and how (step 4). Each of these steps uncovers insights into the challenges in the relationship and reveals the way forward, sometimes in surprising ways. In one of the companies we worked with, the root cause of low performance in the strategies building block turned out to be the fact that the supplier had never asked the customer firm for its strategy. It went about course-correcting by arranging for a mutual strategy discussion, and in the end, it had a solid, jointly developed pitch that turned the game in its favor. All these changes came from the simple canvas exercise of understanding what was really going on, and it led to transformative results in a short time.

Step 5: Persuade your stakeholders

In the fifth and final step of the Triple Fit process, you summarize your consolidated Triple Fit findings and pitch them to stakeholders. There are challenges, especially for product-focused companies in shifting to big-picture thinking; that is why it is important to have a simple but powerful story pitch. You must have a compelling message and persuade senior leaders to understand the benefits and risks, adopt the plan, and then fund the associated initiatives.

A compelling Triple Fit story has three elements: First, develop a catchy central message. Second, formulate your decision proposals, investment, and support requests that go beyond your authority into three key asks. And third, for each ask, summarize the consequences of approval or nonapproval. Afterward, develop a five- to ten-minute, high-impact presentation and rehearse your story with sparring partners until you feel comfortable. Ideally, you'll validate your story with someone from your counterpart's organization, or even present it together with your counterpart to the relevant stakeholders. We will take a detailed look at how to pitch a Triple Fit story in chapter 5.

Christine Dickson, Maersk's global key client director in charge of its account with one of its clothing and accessories retailer customers we will call Elegance, was tasked with disrupting Elegance's thirty-year relationship with one of Maersk's shipping-industry competitors. She believed that conducting a Triple Fit analysis of Maersk's work with Elegance would determine where to improve the relationship. As partners they struggled with several Triple Fit components, most notably strategies, relationships, and structures. She also wanted to identify areas where Maersk could cut into its competitor's relationship with the retailer. Dickson knew that she couldn't simply walk into a meeting with Maersk leaders and tell them that she wanted to conduct a Triple Fit analysis with Elegance. Only after developing a clear understanding of what would be involved in such a process was she able to persuade her leadership team to try this new approach.

With her Elegance counterparts, she conducted a detailed cash-flow analysis, which identified opportunities for savings by reducing Elegance's inventory, discounting obsolete clothing lines, and shortening lead times while increasing Elegance's speed to market. She then selected an Elegance warehouse located in the United States to run a proof of concept. Because Covid-19 limited travel and in-person meetings, Maersk flew a drone inside the warehouse to capture potential areas for improvement on video. As a result of Dickson's analysis, Elegance and Maersk developed transparent delivery schedules, priority lane access to warehouse docks, twenty-four-hour processing, and guaranteed delivery, all of which unlocked significant value across the nine Triple Fit building blocks. The initiative reduced Elegance's logistics costs by more than $25 million during the pilot phase, and Maersk increased its revenue and profitability by 300 percent within two years.

Before pitching, run a cross-check of content based on the following three questions:

- What is the game-changer effect that will result from your proposed go-forward plan?

- What would you do or ask for if you and your customer were one company?

- What would a more radical version of your story look like?

For Sonos and Best Buy, the jointly developed mission was to work together as "one company" to better serve their mutual customer, the end consumer. They also made it clear that if they did not proactively align on strategic issues, both sides would lose significant growth opportunities. This, in turn, led to a solid go-to-market plan for them and helped both companies remove significant blocks to revenue growth for retail sales that created mutual business growth for both the companies.

Triple Fit as a Shared Language

What makes the Triple Fit process so effective is that it enables big change quickly through the five simple steps enabling a meaningful conversation between the teams from the supplier and customer firms. The Triple Fit canvas gives companies a shared language to have a deep strategic dialogue and openly discuss their priorities and define a mutual growth road map.

Once a company has performed some first relationship maturity checks with customers, it is ready to define the success criteria for further scaling. The advantage of working with Triple Fit as a framework is threefold. First, it helps to define relationship success from a customer perspective. Second, it enables sellers and buyers to adjust their success criteria to industry characteristics, considering the trends and external forces that are shaping their industries. And finally, the strategic dialogue allows room for incorporating the cultural context in which the two companies are doing business together.

Triple Fit as a shared language
for customer priorities

The five Triple Fit steps lead to identification of value-creation potential in each of the nine building blocks of the canvas; this is best done by better understanding the customer's point of view. While assessing the relationship, understand the customer priorities in each of the building blocks, because that is what defines the right performance criteria. We advise companies to have at least a set of three to five mutually defined characteristics of each building block before proceeding with analyzing the ratings in depth.

Consider the example of Adcubum, a Swiss-based software manufacturer for the insurance industry. When Adcubum introduced the Triple Fit canvas, it started first with an internal rating round of its top ten customers based on our questionnaire (see figure 2-1). Quickly, the company realized that rating the building block "solutions" was somewhat easier to accomplish than the rating of some of the other blocks, that is, "processes," "systems," or "knowledge." To achieve further clarity, Adcubum developed a broader set of success characteristics per building block that described high performance from a customer perspective.

In our work with Adcubum, we advised it to complement these criteria with a five-star rating system that was easy to understand and resembled the commonly used ratings scales from other industries, including hotel star ratings, Amazon reviews, and so on. In the building block "solutions," for example, two of the newly added high-performance criteria were the sharing of technology road maps and mutually agreed cofinancing of prototypes or minimum viable products. Other newly added criteria were, for example, the open sharing of buying forecasts (communication), joint business development (knowledge), or a reconfigured value chain (processes).

In a nutshell, the company expanded its product-centric KPIs to customer-centric KPIs, which represent the flip from a strong focus on value selling to a broader focus on value creation. Strongly supported by its then CEO, Rene Janesch, Adcubum took these characteristics into the customer workshops and validated them after a joint rating with key stakeholders from both sides. This approach complemented the initial reality check of the ten icebreaker questions (see figure 2-1) very well. It also led to a further calibration of industry-relevant success criteria, as well as priceless insights that would not have been obtained from classic market research or product-centric conversations.

Focusing on customer priorities can also mean highlighting the building blocks where the customer is currently driving high-value initiatives. For example, if the customer focus is on seamlessly integrating technology to unlock value, it could mean focusing on the building blocks: strategies (defining a shared purpose and vision to collaborate on next-generation technology development), systems (enabling information transparency between the two companies for faster decision-making), people (developing highly engaged teams with the requisite skills to implement agile business models), and structures (empowering cross-functional teams to deliver on the agreed initiatives). The building blocks complement each other and can be prioritized through the shared language to enable long-term, customer-centric, value cocreation.

Triple Fit as a shared language for industry trends

When two companies engage in a Triple Fit dialogue as the supplier and customer, they also bring into account their respective industrial contexts. While numerous global trends such as technological shifts, including digitalization and AI, climate change and sustainability initiatives, hybrid work, and societal aspirations focused on diversity, equity, and inclusion across industries, each industry or ecosystem faces the headwinds of change in its own way and at its own pace. Supplier and customer firms engaging in a strategic dialogue come to the table with different business models and sources of competitive advantage in their respective industries. The role of Triple Fit is to help identify and develop mutual sources of competitive advantage—areas where they can benefit from jointly developed capabilities and focused initiatives. This is best accomplished when the Triple Fit discussions are customized for different industries and the common underlying themes are identified.

In the case of Schindler, the Swiss manufacturer of elevators, escalators, and walkways, it also paid off to tailor the Triple Fit success criteria to different customer segments and industries. Notably, Schindler is not only selling to real estate owners but also to a variety of influencers such as architects, specifiers, consulting partners, and so on. To acknowledge the complexity of these relationships, Schindler developed specific Triple Fit success criteria for a total of six customer relationship segments. The interesting insight, however, is that still about 70–80 percent of the criteria are similar across client segments. This has helped Schindler develop an advantage in delivering to each of its customers while catering to their respective industries.

Triple Fit as a shared language for cultural contexts

In our research and consulting work, we have found it helpful to consider cultural aspects.[9] But this is not about cultural stereotypes of survey responses, with some cultures being rather outspoken and blunt in their ratings versus others being shyer and more modest in their feedback. Our experience is different and counterintuitive to the B2C experience. Across industries and cultures, we found that, in B2B relationships, getting business results is the universal language. So, no matter whether you are entering a strategic dialogue with B2B customers in Canada, Brazil, France, Germany, Egypt, South Africa, India, China, or Australia, the universal language is always the same. It's all about customer success, financially and beyond. What matters, however, is how you introduce the value of strategic dialogue to customers in different cultures.

Consider the case of Murex, a Paris-based fintech founded in 1986 and a global leader in trading, risk management, and processing solutions for capital markets. At time of writing, Murex has more than 60,000 users, and its integrated platform is used by 65 of the top 100 banks in the world. Murex is focused on differentiating itself from competitors through shared client centricity with the companies it works with. It aims to be an organization that steadily grows collaborations with diverse clients and furthers shared value creation.

Murex found that the Triple Fit canvas was naturally aligned with its history and its future growth alongside its partner community. In a first round of Triple Fit customer discussions, Murex piloted related initiatives for a select group of customers in New York, Paris, and Singapore, where the company operates global hubs. Analyzing the results of pilot efforts around Triple Fit Strategy, Murex sales leaders quickly understood that securing customer buy-in was key.

Keeping cultural context top of mind, Murex adapted the Triple Fit approach so that account managers employed appropriate methods of contact. In some countries, this simply meant that client executives sent a Triple Fit questionnaire to clients. In others, a first contact by the regional head was more appropriate—a senior stakeholder was best-placed to explain the importance of the upcoming feedback round and client benefits. Sometimes, close multilateral dialog was preferred—client executives from Murex sat with key client stakeholders to come to mutual agreement.

In South Korea, for example, Murex first approached a key customer with the Triple Fit questionnaire. Building on initial client feedback, account manager Ho Sung Lee and his team went through the five steps of the Triple Fit process and then presented their Triple Fit story to the client. They focused on how its international subsidiaries and branches could leverage existing software licenses better. The proposed Triple Fit road map for joint value creation illustrated how the bank could perform profitable trading in their overseas entities as well. In the end, the bank was able to realize significant value gains with minimal investments within a short timeframe by employing the proposed Triple Fit strategy from Murex.

Another example is the case of a Middle East–based real-estate company. When we worked with this client, its mission was to develop a smart city of the future that is also attractive to expats. A Triple Fit workshop helped the development teams to strengthen the relationships with current and future tenants and orchestrate value creation in more concrete terms.

Thus, Triple Fit as a shared language applies across industry and cultural contexts. Sonos and Best Buy had lost that shared language but found it again through the Triple Fit process and were able to align on the value-creation activities necessary to create growth and thus successfully transform their relationship from a transactional one into a strategic partnership. To sum up, strategic dialogue works best with a shared language that you have with your customers through the five Triple Fit process steps; it is one of the most critical conversations in shaping your mutual strategy and turning sticky roadblocks into new opportunities. In the next chapter, we will learn how the insights from this dialogue can be developed into defining game-changer strategies.

TAKEAWAYS

- High-performing business relationships start with a broader conversation about how both parties can shape the future together—the strategic dialogue.

- The Triple Fit process consists of five key steps to enable this dialogue for joint value creation:

    1. Assess where the relationship stands

    2. Identify areas for improvement

    3. Develop workable solutions

    4. Differentiate between long- and short-term actions

    5. Persuade your stakeholders

- Triple Fit serves as a shared language for identifying and incorporating customer priorities, industry trends, and cultural contexts in which two companies operate.

REFLECTION QUESTIONS

- Which of your customers do you already engage with in a strategic dialogue?

- How many of them would give you five-star ratings? Download the free questionnaire from triplefitstrategy.com and conduct a first evaluation of the relationship performance.

- What do your industry-specific success criteria look like for the nine Triple Fit building blocks?

CHAPTER 3

DEFINE GAME-CHANGERS

A few years ago, a global defense technology and services company, one of our clients that we'll call Parabellum, faced a crossroads. On one hand, Parabellum enjoyed long-term government contracts with its home country's armed forces. On the other hand, Parabellum was also actively selling its products and services to military and civilian organizations across industries and countries around the globe. In both cases, Parabellum relied heavily on the strong personal relationships it had built with key decision-makers over decades.

However, a first Triple Fit analysis of its sales plans showed something less well conceived and intentional. The account plans often resembled customer annual reports with lots of irrelevant general data. The strategy part of account plans (if existent) was mostly mere wish lists or at best sales extrapolations, none of which had customers validated. An often-heard phrase was: "Our strategy is to remain (or become) the number one supplier." With all due respect, this is not a strategy, but a sales objective.[1]

When a tough economy emerged, Parabellum's customers started to look more closely at their contracts and service agreements. As a consequence, Parabellum was losing business at a clip at which it had never lost business before, and it needed to understand why and stop the exodus. The company focused first on shoring up its most important customer relationships.

To support these efforts, Parabellum's management launched a Triple Fit program to get things back on track. After two years of Triple Fit activities, however, the efforts showed mixed results. In some cases, the outcomes of the first strategic customer dialogues exceeded expectations, while in others, they fell behind. In one case, the business took off from less than €1 million to more than €10 million with a shared investment at a favorable margin. In another case, the customer contact from procurement simply refused to talk about value beyond volume discounts.

Investigating the situation further, Parabellum's sales leaders learned that despite a few breakthroughs, real game-changer ideas and initiatives were almost nonexistent. Notably, broader business development thinking was missing in both the military and the civilian business relationships. In particular, the implementation of the strategic customer dialogue had greatly slowed down due to a strong pushback from multiple levels of Parabellum's own sales organization. The main reason was the sales team's strong internal belief that customers had to buy Parabellum's products and services anyway due to long-term contractual agreements. In some cases, the account managers and team leaders in charge actively sabotaged the initiation of a strategic dialogue, as they could simply not imagine the value of an unscripted discussion via a Triple Fit process.

Only when the management started to assign the lead to new and more customer-centric-minded account managers and sales leaders did things start to change. Step-by-step, the company started to make substantial progress and won, for example, prestigious contracts with organizations such as NASA and Boeing. As in the previously introduced cases, the secret of success was to broaden the focus from the solutions building block to all nine building blocks of the Triple Fit canvas.

Today—more than five years after the initial effort—Parabellum still uses the Triple Fit canvas to initiate game-changers for relationship breakthroughs, both from recurring sales and new business development perspectives. The lesson from the Parabellum case is rather simple—don't underestimate the power of the internal comfort zone, as it could significantly delay (or even kill) the game-changers that will lead to future business opportunities.

Sales Needs a New Perspective

With a two-year delay, Parabellum finally achieved its sales goals because it shifted from selling products and services to orchestrating value creation by initiating game-changers for its clients. In our research and advisory work, however, we have encountered multiple cases where companies deliberately killed future business opportunities and stayed away from game-changer ideas and initiatives. Consequently, they left a lot of money on the table because of a shortsighted and narrow view on sales. Theoretically speaking, not entering a strategic dialogue with customers and not caring about developing lasting business relationships is also an option. But practically speaking, the question remains how wise and profitable such a move really is.

Consider, for example, the case of another client we worked with that we'll call Global Bathroom Systems (GBS). GBS sold its products mostly via distributors and, hence, had a great need to align its sales and marketing activities for its sales channel. At the same time, however, GBS employees did not regard their counterparts at the distributor side as equals. They often referred to them as "bandits" who only existed to steal their margins and create win-lose scenarios. As top management did not intervene, the level of strategic discussions with clients was low and, in many cases, simply missing. To make up for this deficit in game-changer conversations, GBS turned to creating a strong marketing pull for its new products and spending millions of dollars to convince end consumers of its superior technology.

The saddest part of the story, however, is that GBS had all the information to change the game in its hands before it took misguided actions. In a series of Triple Fit workshops, the company accurately identified strengths and weaknesses in its major relationships with distributors and customers across geographies. But instead of push-ing for the game-changers to create value for significant relationship breakthroughs, the company deliberately chose to double-down on product-centric marketing efforts. A recent retrospective on publicly available business results revealed that competitors seeking a stron-ger strategic dialogue with the "bandits" scored higher growth and profit rates, despite all of GBS's consumer-pull efforts. Imagine the business potential that GBS could have tapped into, if it had shifted its costly marketing and value-selling approach to a broader value-creation approach and gone into a deeper, more strategic dialogue with its customers. Let alone if GBS had implemented a more collabo-rative perspective toward its distributor relationships—potentially a true game-changer, but a missed opportunity.

Parabellum eventually mastered the transition to a more customer-centric approach and could access and unlock more promising growth opportunities than before despite all the challenges and dynamics of the global defense industry. GBS, on the other hand, chose to stay with the initial product-selling focus. It is still in business, but despite a Covid-19-driven spike in its industry, it is facing limited growth opportunities.

But now, fasten your seatbelts. The cases of Parabellum and GBS are just two of countless difficult transformation examples we have witnessed in our training and advisory work. The reality we see in our fieldwork looks often even worse, mainly driven by a negotiation mindset instead of a value cocreation perspective.

Consider the case of a large global company in the food processing industry that we call Cartagena. When Cartagena's sales reps and ac-count managers were going through a Triple Fit exercise, the company was coming from a dominant market position and had a strong focus on creating high-quality products and delivering sales growth. How-ever, Cartagena's sales reps found themselves stuck in the triangle of sales, strongly focused on delivering high performance in three build-ing blocks: people, relationships, and knowledge. They were mainly acting as skilled negotiators with deep product expertise calling on a

procurement counterpart but unable to address the total business perspective required to orchestrate value for mutual growth. They lacked
the clarity and motivation to address the gaps in other building blocks
such as strategies, processes, systems, structures, and the like because
they felt disempowered to influence any game-changer actions in these
areas. In addition, to conquer greater market share, the organization
encouraged product-centric strategies that were not validated by Cartagena's top customers. The triangle of sales focus clearly hindered the
company from getting closer to their customers. (See figure 3-1.)

Only when the company started to lose out against more agile,
customer-centric competitors did it start to take corrective actions.
A cornerstone action was the focus on customers with the highest
growth potential and winning back market share from competitors via
a Triple Fit growth program. The company trained its top thirty strategic account managers in the total business perspective that included
all Triple Fit building blocks. As a part of that training, all thirty of
their respective teams reached out to the customers and validated a
game plan for mutual growth beyond the triangle of sales. They implemented a fast-track delivery channel to meet customers' requests
for new product development and emergency spare part services for
food-processing machines as a key step in innovating their processes.

FIGURE 3-1

Triangle of sales perspective versus total business perspective

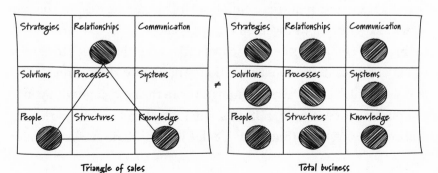

Triangle of sales   Total business

To address organizational structures, they elevated the position of the account managers to a more empowered ownership role. They also addressed strategic gaps by aligning sustainability initiatives and goals in response to strong customer expectations. Finally, they exchanged knowledge with the customers to jointly identify total cost of ownership savings of €5 million in the pilot project alone. By mastering the shift from the narrow triangle of sales to a total business perspective, Cartagena got closer to its customers which turned around the situation and brought its business back on the growth track.

Finding Your Game-Changer

We define a game-changer as a radically different way of looking at business relationships and orchestrating a collaboration. Game-changer ideas or initiatives create real growth based on a solid, long-term perspective of the customer relationship and mutual efforts by both sides. It also requires an understanding of what it will take to execute this initiative, with strategic clarity that cuts through complexity. In a world where even the best strategies frequently fall short on execution, there is no better way to ensure successful execution than by forging it together with the customer.[2] That is exactly what changes the playing field and, hence, the game.

We also need to know what a game-changer is *not*. A game-changer is not a shiny new idea or strategic plan that looks like the old one with new packaging. It requires a mindset shift based on discovering answers to key questions together with customers. It also requires recognizing your company's existing capabilities and what needs to change to make the next strategic transition. And finally, it requires understanding which customers are going to be in the new game with you.

Consider, for example, a US-based manufacturer of drug packaging and delivery systems that we will call Flexilis. Olivia[*], then a Flexilis

---

* Name disguised.

account manager, discovered that the business with its key client we will call Remedium could run into severe problems due to so-called "legacy established products." Some of the products that Flexilis was supplying to Remedium were more than forty years old and contained dry natural rubber (DNR). As the US Food and Drug Administration (FDA) regulations for the use of DNR started to change, routine FDA inspections surfaced, increasing issues such as potential allergic reactions. In blunt terms, some of these products were about to become a time bomb with an unclear end scenario.

Anticipating the worst-case scenario ahead of time, Olivia used a Triple Fit process to analyze the situation in more detail. The customer ratings across the nine building blocks spanned from one to three stars only—a clear indicator that things needed to be fixed on several fronts. Together with a core team of Flexilis and Remedium stakeholders, she identified two high priority areas to work on further. The first area covered the three building blocks strategies, relationships, and communication at the planning fit level. The second included the two building blocks solutions and processes at the execution fit level (see figure 3-2).

FIGURE 3-2

Triple Fit results for Flexilis and Remedium at the start and one year later

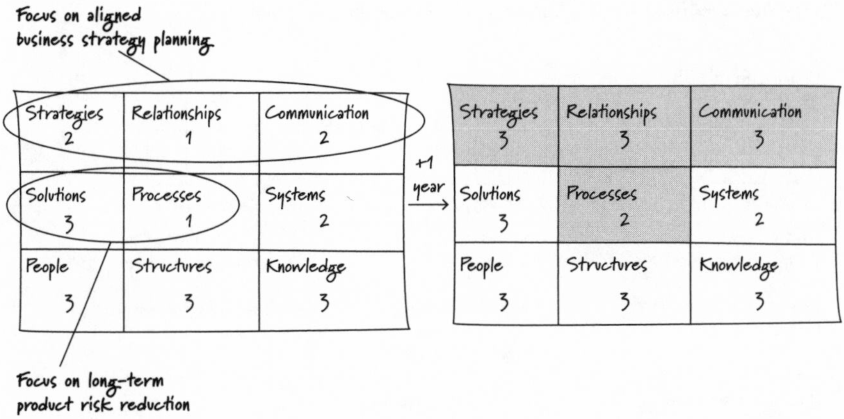

Focus on aligned business strategy planning

Focus on long-term product risk reduction

To speed up the traditionally slow decision-making processes at both companies and understanding that she did not have unlimited time to address the product-risk, Olivia developed a two-pronged strategy to address both issues in parallel while acknowledging different timelines for each. In combination, both would be the backbone for a game-changer that she called "jointly de-risking business." She recognized that if she didn't save this business, the account would likely never recover, but if she could preserve Remedium's multi-million dollar business just until Flexilis could transition its product line, she'd not only preserve the customer's business but open much more business for Flexilis because of newer, modern product formulations that met FDA requirements. It was the tip of the proverbial iceberg. Saving this deal would be a game-changer. One year later, new Triple Fit ratings showed significant improvements, and eight years after the initial idea, the partnership is still running on track.

Similarly, in the Maersk and Kotahi example, the process that both teams used in the Copenhagen workshop followed the Triple Fit process sequence presented in chapter 2. Both teams took the time to investigate the ratings before meeting in person. To identify hidden game-changer ideas, both parties found it helpful to revisit the Triple

FIGURE 3-3

Deep-dive questions for evaluating performance in the planning fit

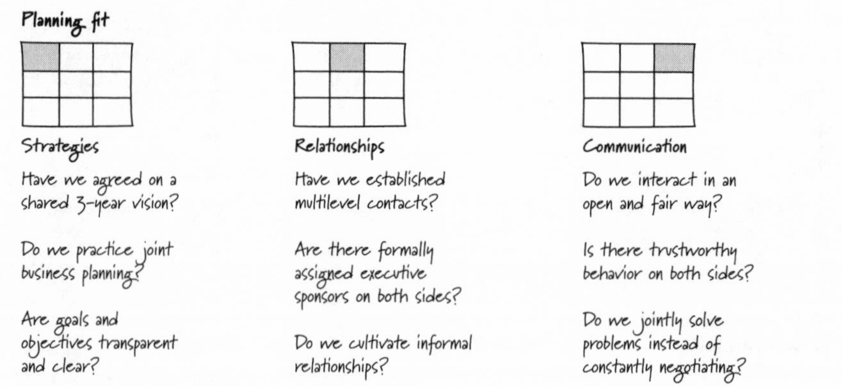

Planning fit

Strategies

Have we agreed on a shared 3-year vision?

Do we practice joint business planning?

Are goals and objectives transparent and clear?

Relationships

Have we established multilevel contacts?

Are there formally assigned executive sponsors on both sides?

Do we cultivate informal relationships?

Communication

Do we interact in an open and fair way?

Is there trustworthy behavior on both sides?

Do we jointly solve problems instead of constantly negotiating?

FIGURE 3-4

Deep-dive questions for evaluating performance in the execution fit

Execution fit

Solutions

Have we developed a tailored value proposition?

Do we share technology road maps?

Do we have full visibility of long-term joint growth potential?

Processes

Are roles and responsibilities clearly defined on both sides?

Have we optimized activity along the value chain?

Do we share mission critical information?

Systems

Are our IT systems integrated?

Do we apply joint financial KPIs and business scorecards?

Do we share financial risks and rewards approved by legal?

Fit ratings based on a broader set of questions to ensure a common understanding and shared language for value cocreation. To support the calibration of in-depth Triple Fit discussions, the Maersk-Kotahi team looked into popular characteristics that describe a five-star performance. Figures 3-3, 3-4, and 3-5 describe these characteristics in nine questions per Triple Fit level.

FIGURE 3-5

Deep-dive questions for evaluating performance in the resources fit

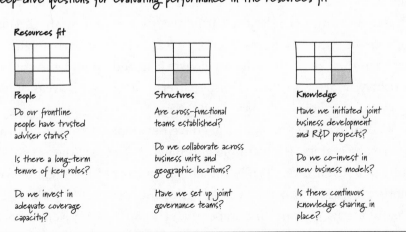

Resources fit

People

Do our frontline people have trusted adviser status?

Is there a long-term tenure of key roles?

Do we invest in adequate coverage capacity?

Structures

Are cross-functional teams established?

Do we collaborate across business units and geographic locations?

Have we set up joint governance teams?

Knowledge

Have we initiated joint business development and R&D projects?

Do we co-invest in new business models?

Is there continuous knowledge sharing in place?

These questions greatly helped the Maersk-Kotahi team to further understand the other party's point of view, not necessarily always leading to an agreement, but surely creating transparency about the underlying motivation and intention in jointly agreed priority areas. Both teams also agreed to update Triple Fit ratings on an annual basis, resulting in solid improvements in formerly weak areas within some few ninety-day quick-win cycles. These ninety-day cycles provided the foundations to achieve several significant outcomes including establishing a joint operations team focused on new areas of efficiency improvements, extending the depth of the relationship with Kotahi's shareholders to trial new Maersk capability for in-market logistics, quick wins for sharing data across respective digital ecosystems and a long-term green fuel enabled sustainability roadmap.

But most importantly, both teams embedded the Triple Fit process as a key part in their business process. Supervised by the executive sponsors of the business relationship—in this case, the CEOs from both sides, David Ross and Vincent Clerc—both companies felt ready to embark on a joint game-changer journey for the next decade.

Identifying Game-Changer Patterns

Triple Fit deep-dive discussions can surface game-changer ideas and initiatives for individual customer relationships. But what if you manage not only one relationship but ten, twenty, or a hundred? How do you find game-changers then? One way is to let everybody figure out their own ideas, as in the previously featured examples. Another, probably smarter way, is to look at patterns of Triple Fit areas of improvement, or hot issues, as we call them.

To capture these insights, we have developed a tool called the hot issues matrix. It's a simple approach that consolidates the results of a given set of Triple Fit canvas ratings into a higher-level picture by presenting the average rating for each building block. To ensure a true outside-in perspective, the ratings entered in each

Triple Fit canvas *must come from the customer, and not from the supplier.* The aggregated results that are displayed in the hot issues matrix are a great way to emphasize customer priorities that lead to the identification of game-changers. Next, we describe how the hot issues matrix works in simple graphical steps to use yourself (see figure 3-6).

The underlying assumption is that if you have a portfolio of business relationships, it is likely that you are going to see some patterns of high-, medium-, or low-performing building blocks. The purpose of this analysis is to identify relationship risks that could affect the whole organization.

The consolidated Triple Fit data provides a fact-based view of hot issues across the selected relationships and enables you to focus on those areas that need substantial improvement from a managerial perspective. You may also want to use the generated insights to cross-check the progress of other, ongoing major initiatives in your organization. If necessary, use the results to take corrective action or accelerate the implementation pace further.

FIGURE 3-6

Consolidating Triple Fit ratings with the hot issues matrix

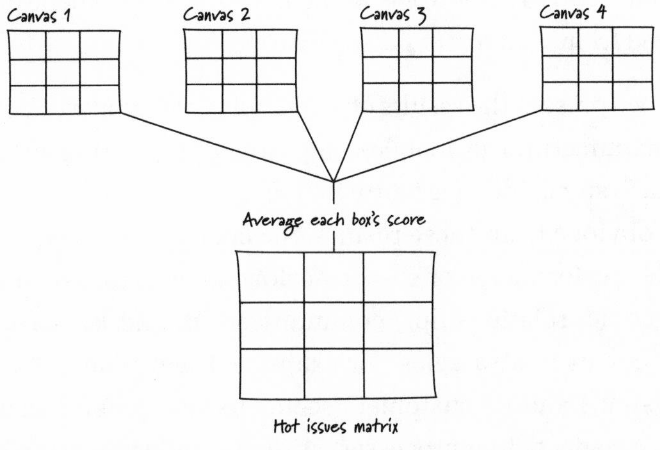

Hot issues matrix

The following steps help to perform a hot issues analysis:

1. Select the relationships you want to analyze

2. Plot the customer-validated ratings in the hot issues matrix

3. Define priority areas (usually building blocks with average ratings of 2.5 or lower)

4. Set a "to-be status" for each priority area (i.e., a rating should improve from 1.8 to 3.0)

5. Analyze each priority area along the sequence "facts–conclusions–consequences"

6. Summarize your findings in a set of game-changer ideas and initiatives

For a first interpretation of a hot issues matrix and the prioritization of Triple Fit building blocks, you may want to ask the following questions:

- What are the strengths of the selected relationship portfolio?

- What are the weaknesses of the selected relationship portfolio?

- Can we see patterns across individual Triple Fit canvas ratings?

- Which two to three areas would most likely need to be prioritized from a customer perspective?

Next, we present the results of a first hot issues analysis from a US-based manufacturer of mobile computing and printing systems we call Data Systems Inc. (see figure 3-7).

As is obvious from these results, the customers of Data Systems value the performance of classic performance areas, such as solutions, people, relationships, communication, and knowledge. But when it comes to strategies, for example, the disconnect between Data Systems and its customers seems to be a general issue. Furthermore, aspects like processes, systems, and structures are also

FIGURE 3-7

Hot issues matrix example of Data Systems Inc.

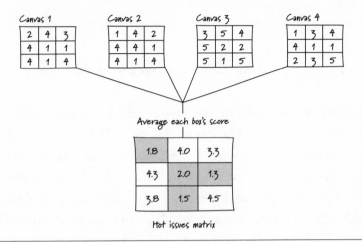

Hot issues matrix

rated low, especially in comparison with the other factors. Referring to the previous discussion about selling products versus orchestrating value creation, one could conclude that Data Systems does a great job in selling its products but misses value-creation opportunities beyond the traditionally important success factors in the industry. To differentiate itself from competition and exploit further growth potential, Data Systems should develop game-changers in the building blocks strategies, processes, systems, and structures. In order to do this, we recommend completing a simple "facts–conclusions–consequences" sequence for each of these four building blocks starting with stating observed facts, continued with drawing relevant conclusions, and ending with necessary consequences for actions.

Of course, one could also leave this interpretation to each sales rep individually and hope for breakthroughs. But hope is not a good strategy in sales, so having the big-picture view of where business relationships with customers that are stalling will generate two positive effects: First, it makes senior leaders immediately aware of the favorable conditions for success only they can provide. And second, the sales team members can learn from each other and share experiences and best practices as they go forward without losing time with lone-wolf initiatives.

Taking Game-Changers to the Next Level

But the interpretation of hot issues results doesn't stop here. Consider, for example, the case of one of our clients, a Big Four audit company we call Auditorium. A few years ago, Auditorium was preparing for a significant transition in European Union rules for accounting, the so-called Mandatory Audit Firm Rotation, to be completed in 2026. In a nutshell, Auditorium was soon about to lose about half of its top customers but at the same time was eligible to pitch to new customers that were previously audited by one of its competitors.[3] The company used Triple Fit workshops to evaluate the status of its relationships with its top fifty European clients. The analysis of the individual and consolidated Triple Fit results revealed two interesting patterns:

1. Auditorium's own sales team members rated the firm's Triple Fit performance consistently higher than their clients' performance.

2. The consolidated client ratings showed strong improvement potential across almost the whole Triple Fit canvas.

These are stark and challenging results for a Triple Fit exercise. To see such consistent patterns and with no particularly strong points—just consistent disconnect with clients across all nine sectors—forced Auditorium to confront a harsh reality. But before acting, the company first deeply reflected through heavy internal debates designed to define a path forward that would sync its ratings with its clients and create strong sectors of performance on the Triple Fit canvas.

The firm decided to tackle the Triple Fit deficits step-by-step. Formulating a target ambition for Triple Fit ratings three years out,

FIGURE 3-8

Auditorium's three-year master plan for organizational change

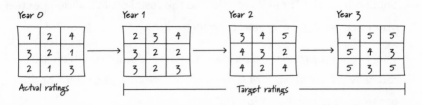

Year 0		
1	2	4
3	2	1
2	1	3

Actual ratings

Year 1		
2	3	4
3	2	2
3	2	3

Year 2		
3	4	5
4	3	2
4	2	4

Year 3		
4	5	5
5	4	3
5	3	5

Target ratings

Auditorium embarked on a three-year transformation program. Figure 3-8 illustrates the master plan.

The initiative started with a focus on the building blocks people, strategies, and relationships for year one. In year two, the focus would shift to processes, systems, and structures, while the work on the other aspects from year one would continue. In year three, the ambition was to get to a level that was far above the ratings of year zero—also acknowledging that not all clients would have achieved five-star ratings at the same time for the same building blocks until then. A key success factor was that Auditorium agreed to implement game-changers at both the individual and organizational levels. Thus, the client managers had the freedom to maneuver despite corporate initiatives, such as a stronger push of new consulting service offerings in case of the loss of a 100-year-old audit mandate. After three years, the efforts have paid off, and Auditorium could not only keep a good number of client relationships that were at risk but also took the results to a global level and embarked on a follow-up program that aimed at an ongoing strategic dialogue with its most important clients.

While there are uncertainties and risks in defining a game-changer approach at the organizational level, the upside can be so strategically significant for a company that failing to pursue a possible game-changer can be nothing less than a huge missed opportunity. In the next chapter, we will take these ideas into the implementation stage even further and identify the growth trajectories that apply to the entire portfolio, leading to transformative results on a larger scale.

TAKEAWAYS

- Shifting from the "triangle of sales" to the "total business" perspective opens up new value-creation opportunities.

- The Triple Fit process helps identify game-changers, which are radically different ways of looking at business relationships and orchestrating collaboration with customers.

- Identifying hot issues across the selected relationships allows companies to focus on those areas that need substantial improvement from a customer perspective.

REFLECTION QUESTIONS

- What is your and your sales team's dominant perspective: triangle of sales or total business perspective?

- Which building blocks hinder the total business perspective and can benefit from game-changers through the Triple Fit process?

- What would your hot issues based on estimated or actual Triple Fit ratings from your top ten customers look like? Go to triplefitstrategy.com for further resources on hot issues.

NAVIGATING TRIPLE FIT JOURNEYS

CHAPTER 4

FOCUS WHERE THE GROWTH IS

Part I of this book was about customer-centricity and an introduction to the Triple Fit process, with three fit levels and five steps and how it leads to developing game-changers that are based on value-creation opportunities. In part II, we go to the next level by putting the process into action in the real world and making customer-centric business growth a reality. We will show how companies can navigate the growth journey through five strategic moves, despite adversarial conditions. As in the previous chapters, we will give real-life examples and practical steps to initiate and maintain the growth momentum.

When Jose Varela, then vice president and general manager strategic sourcing and packaging solutions at 3M, was at a meeting with BASF, one of his strategic suppliers, he challenged it with a request: "You are already one of our top suppliers globally. But if you really want to differentiate BASF, help us grow in Asia." After a pause, he added, "With suppliers, we spend 90 percent of our time managing transactions, and 10 percent on growing. We want to invert that." Alan Weinstein, then a global account manager at BASF based in Ohio, and responsible for managing the entire relationship with its customer 3M, began weighing his options together with us.

On the one hand, he could offer a compelling value proposition for the products that best fit the target region and the corresponding country markets. Flanked with a heavy sales-push initiative executed by the regional sales force, this approach had always delivered some results in the past. On the other hand, he could conduct further target market research to understand the needs of 3M's customer segments. Building on these results, he could launch marketing-pull activities to drive 3M's willingness to use BASF ingredients in its products. While both approaches have merits, both address the growth challenge only from an inside-out perspective.

Connect the Dots for Breakthroughs

After twenty-four hours of reflection, Weinstein opted for a third option. He decided to involve the customer from an outside-in perspective from the very beginning. Fast-forward two years and 3M's business supported by BASF products had doubled, and BASF had added $50 million of recurring sales to the existing business. In addition, BASF won the 3M Supplier of the Year Award in 2018 and 2020. So what was its secret to success? How did the two companies drive growth above average in the short and long terms? And, particularly, which areas of the Triple Fit canvas were they focusing on?

Based on their analysis, Varela and Weinstein realized that the additional value BASF could bring to the table for 3M was not primarily groundbreaking science for new products. On the contrary, they noted, it was all about establishing a global commercial innovation network to drive both companies' further business growth. Their conclusion was driven by the analysis of the initial Triple Fit canvas for 3M Asia (see figure 4-1). As you can see, there were solid performance ratings for the building blocks "structure" and "systems." This was, in fact, good news, as it meant that important business enablers at the execution and resources fit levels were already in place. What was missing, however, was the alignment at the planning fit level, combined with a low rating for "solutions." Having two-star ratings

FIGURE 4-1

Initial Triple Fit ratings for the BASF—3M case

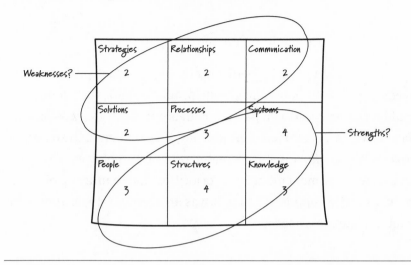

across the whole planning fit implied huge improvement potential, and this was the trigger for Weinstein and Varela's conclusion.

Together with the regional teams in Asia, they identified sources of value beyond the classic product-market it. A key component for success was sharing and aligning strategies via increased executive relationships, facilitating the dialogue between 3M's headquarters and the region, and communicating implementation plans to all functions. Furthermore, they were launching commercially viable pilot projects for 3M key product areas, coordinating investments from both sides in new technologies, and sharing resources to manage the growing business pipeline for mutual success.

Leverage the Triple Fit Principles

Knowing that they were in for the long term, Weinstein and Varela also crafted a mutually agreed, three-year collaboration road map for further growth. The road map development was based on three Triple Fit principles featured in chapter 1. For illustrative purposes, we bring them back, so you can follow the working process that helped Varela and Weinstein to connect the dots for the first breakthrough.

Principle 1: Realign your planning

Planning should not only focus on aligning product pitches to the buyer's needs or on polishing a value proposition for the products. It should focus on creating a partner collaboration strategy. When Varela and Weinstein started their journey, they realigned the planning between both companies for greater proximity between key functions, faster alignment of business priorities, and seamless global and regional service support. In fact, it was all about strategic alignment for mutual business success.

Principle 2: Reconfigure your execution

After getting the planning fit level in order, both companies moved to the execution fit level. Again, it was essential to prioritize activities and secure investments for fast breakthroughs. Based on 3M's guidance on priority growth platforms in Asia, both companies focused on quick wins that created mutual growth, while at the same time building an increasing project pipeline for long-term growth. For the short term, this meant, for example, not immediately involving all of BASF's twelve divisions. It also meant limiting the execution efforts to commercialize new ideas to only three of 3M's many divisions—medical solutions, automotive and aerospace, and industrial adhesives and tapes. Therefore, both partners achieved the first breakthroughs in the range of $5 million in the first twelve months, followed by even higher numbers in later years.

Principle 3: Reallocate your resources

Finally, both companies agreed on a new view of resource allocation. Varela at 3M, for example, committed to invest in two new roles on its side—a key supplier manager and a global R&D manager. For cost reasons, both roles were not exclusively dedicated to the BASF relationship. But they greatly helped to steer the activities in the right way and, for example, drove collaboration across regions and product categories. BASF, in turn, named Weinstein the global commercial innovation network leader, supported by three colleagues in the main global regions. Together with the local teams and executive sponsors, both companies leveraged each other's resources for mutually beneficial growth. Looking back on the two first years of the closer collaboration, Kevin Twohy, director of sourcing operations at 3M, reflected: "BASF's approach to building our relationship across functions is extremely innovative and a differentiator versus the competition."[1]

Replicate for Sustainable Growth

In the traditional B2B selling logic, growth usually happens either via heavy sales-push initiatives such as aggressive sales promotion and discount campaigns, or market-pull activities such as account-based marketing and other smart end-user targeting activities. The BASF–3M example shows that there is a third way: collaborating strategically. When awarding the second supplier award in a row to BASF in 2021, Debora Fronczak, then senior vice president and chief procurement officer at 3M, said, "Supplier collaboration is critical to supply chain success. We are fortunate to work with great suppliers who are committed to fostering a relationship with 3M. These collaborative relationships help us to serve our customers with innovative and valuable solutions."[2] As a consequence, BASF enjoyed a yearly CAGR of 15 percent with the 3M business over the next three years.

Of course, leveraging the Triple Fit principles won't always be easy or yield results overnight. But the 3M case shows that fast growth in B2B sales is enabled by a stronger commercial perspective instead of a pure technology focus. After evaluating the experiences of the 3M relationship, BASF launched in 2019 a new global strategy that includes a series of customer networks with strong executive support to drive further growth with more customers.

Consider, for example, the case of BASF's customer Natura & Co., a Brazilian global personal care cosmetics group headquartered in São Paulo. The Natura group brands currently include Natura Cosméticos, The Body Shop, and Avon Products. In 2022, Fabiane Martins became global key account manager at BASF for Natura and we were coaching her and her team to take the relationship with Natura to the next level. Building on the same Triple Fit principles that her colleague Alan Weinstein used for 3M, she approached her counterparts at Natura from procurement to R&D to prioritize mutual growth opportunities. In total, Martins held eleven Triple Fit interviews of thirty to forty-five minutes each. On the one hand, this may sound like a lot of extra work. On the other, it allowed her to pool the results and identify the key pattern that spanned a master Triple Fit canvas across all eleven documented talks. BASF and Natura then focused on two Triple Fit building blocks—strategies and solutions—to take the relationship to the next level and help each other to grow in Asia.

Martins' team also worked in ninety-day Triple Fit implementation cycles and established a customer-validated, fast-track growth plan in less than nine months. Progress was presented to stakeholders from both companies regularly to keep the top ten projects on track and decide on key investments on an ongoing basis, rather than once per year. Within a year after the start of the Triple Fit discussions with BASF, Natura had benefited in multiple ways. Natura was able to identify additional sales potential in the range of a market size of more than $100 million, and project higher profits opportunities due to ongoing go-to-market support in a key growth category, as well as a significant contribution to Natura's 2030 sustainability agenda. BASF in turn benefited financially with an increased sales pipeline of more than $10 million recurring business per year, a much more robust business relationship, and with a shared language for new business development across functions and regions to reallocate resources to other, promising customer relationships for business breakthroughs.[3]

The BASF example showed that finding a shared language for mutual growth was the key to success. Zeroing in on the underperforming areas of the Triple Fit canvas helped find the drivers for 3M's growth and reallocate resources for breakthroughs. We admit that the need for resource allocation is not a new insight. The global business environment has always required companies to divert their resources to pursue new opportunities and manage risks. Often, this has meant a refocus on customer sectors that are doing well, while managing the investments in the customer sectors that are facing a slowdown. These changes can demand the addition of new products and services to the pipeline or the pursuit of different customer segments, while also transforming the processes and systems that enable the delivery of the products and services to their business customers. Consequently, the need to invent new business models together increases. Thus, the business landscape requires companies to adjust their strategic focus by refocusing their efforts for organic growth or engaging in acquisitions or alliances to add to their portfolio. This seemed to be the golden rule to unlock growth, while making intelligent decisions at the strategy-execution level to ensure superior financial returns and competitive advantage.

Leading business-to-business players focus on using data and analytics to build a growth engine that propels their organizations from merely generating insights to delivering impact with their customers. This applies to both scenarios of organic business growth, through unlocking new opportunities in existing or new markets, and inorganic growth, through mergers and acquisitions, for any given organization with the goal to grow fast and sustainably.[4] However, to plan for future growth, companies have typically looked to their past performance to prepare forecasting models.[5] But when it comes to predicting growth with customers, even with the most advanced analytics, the visibility into the future remains limited, as past data is only descriptive and not prescriptive.[6] But what can you do when your company is in uncharted territory while identifying new growth areas with the customers? Where can you focus when more of the same old-style selling is not yielding the envisioned results? BASF and 3M answered these questions in a new, forward-looking way that was beneficial for that one case. But how do you get insights across one example and even industries? Are there any strategic moves that help companies create profitable and sustainable growth with their customers?

The Booster Zone Grid

In order to answer the above questions, and derive the strategic moves that can create breakthrough results for the high-performing business relationships with predictive information, we launched a series of research consortia with over a hundred companies across industries and geographies.[7]

For each company in each consortium, we collected the meta data for the top customer relationships based on the Triple Fit framework and validated by customers. We then calculated the Triple Fit performance of the selected customer relationships based on the sum of all nine Triple Fit ratings as a measure of the quality of the customer relationship between two firms, as depicted in figure 4-2.

FIGURE 4-2

Triple Fit performance calculation

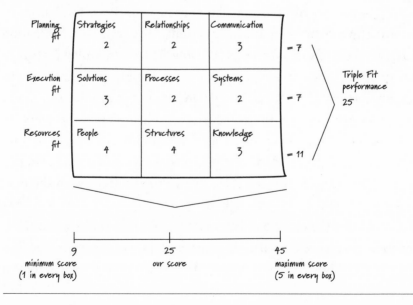

Along with the Triple Fit performance, the supplier firm needs to measure the business potential with its customer. Based on our research, this is best measured through the so-called share of wallet, defined as the supplier firm's percentage share of its customer's accessible market spending. In other words, the total wallet size for the products and services currently offered in the supplier firm's portfolio. The share of wallet is usually measured as a percentage ranging from 0 to 100 percent (see figure 4-3).

Over the years, our work has surfaced two scenarios to calculate the share of wallet. If the relationship is defined by one product or service (mono-product) or spans one single market such as one country, then scenario one is applicable. If there are several products (multi-product) or markets and geographies in play, scenario two is more realistic. A caveat: just as the ratings for the Triple Fit performance are still carrying some personally driven perceptions, so also the share-of-wallet figures are driven partly by perception and won't be precise. But they will offer guidance. It makes a huge difference if your share of wallet is 20 percent or 80 percent.

A recent incident in a workshop may help us better understand the previous two scenarios. After the introduction of the Triple Fit

FIGURE 4-3

Share-of-wallet calculation and scenarios

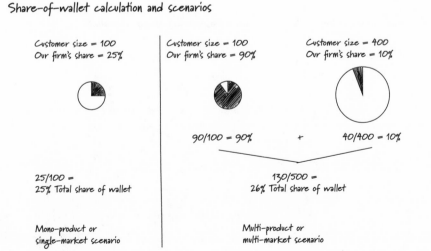

Customer size = 100
Our firm's share = 25%

Customer size = 100
Our firm's share = 90%

Customer size = 400
Our firm's share = 10%

90/100 = 90%   +   40/400 = 10%

25/100 =
25% Total share of wallet

130/500 =
26% Total share of wallet

Mono-product or
single-market scenario

Multi-product or
multi-market scenario

process and the share-of-wallet definition, a longtime account manager aggressively criticized us. He had been responsible for a key account relationship for more than twenty years and was working hard
to keep the business on track. When we questioned his growth potential calculation, he smashed the customers' procurement manual on
the table and said, "The customer has stated a clear multi-supplier
strategy, where no supplier will get more than 25 percent share of
wallet! I am already at 30 percent, so leave me alone and let me do my
job!" A bit stunned, we noted that there was indeed a 25 percent rule
mentioned in the manual. But when we then confronted the customer's procurement head directly about the manual information, he re-
plied, with a smile on his face, "Well, that's the theory. But in practice,
we have indeed four suppliers, yet the best one gets 80 percent of our
spending. The other three serve as qualified suppliers for security and
excess capacity needs for the remaining 20 percent." And guess what?
The supplier company we were working with was not the number-one
supplier. So in reality, they actually did not have 30 percent but less
than 10 percent of the customer's actual share of wallet.

What helped us to get the furious account manager back on track
was a graphical assessment measuring Triple Fit performance (TFP)
on the x-axis and share of wallet (SOW) on the y-axis (see figure 4-4).

FIGURE 4-4

The correlation between Triple Fit performance and share of wallet

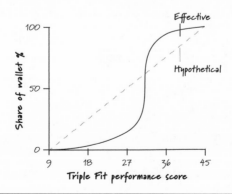

Working with the consortium data, we hypothesized a linear correlation between TFP and SOW. Following the motto "more is better," we were assuming that higher performance leads to higher share of wallet. But contrary to our expectations, the data showed an S-curve relationship as follows:[8]

- Triple Fit performance between 9 and 27: slow rising slope

- Triple Fit performance between 27 and 36: steep rise in slope

- Triple Fit performance between 36 and 45: flattening slope

This suggests that the goal is not to simply increase the Triple Fit score across the board for every relationship. Rather the strategy will vary depending on where you end up when plotting your share of wallet against the Triple Fit score. We have created the booster zone grid as a tool for the interested reader. The grid can serve as a basis for turbocharging the growth of a company if the focus is on the customers with the highest growth potential and the efforts are focused on these customers for breakthroughs. It can also serve as an early warning system for the entire customer portfolio, as it reveals where most accounts are currently accumulating and highlights the need to bring them closer to the S-curve itself to benefit from the boost effect of the S-curve. In a nutshell, the location of any given customer relationship is a reality check for the current health of that relationship. It also determines the strategic move you may want to make to maximize the value for both parties based on five possible options: improve, protect, boost, maintain, and optimize (see figure 4-5).

The booster zone grid helped BASF, for example, to enter a growth strategy with customers 3M and Natura, as both these customers were positioned on the right edge of the "improve" zone to the "booster" zone with low share-of-wallet percentages and also relatively low Triple Fit performance scores. BASF not only followed the three Triple Fit principles and completed the five steps of the Triple Fit process, but also successfully applied the strategic moves that were revealed by this grid, thus making fast growth possible within a short time.

FIGURE 4-5

The five zones of the booster zone grid

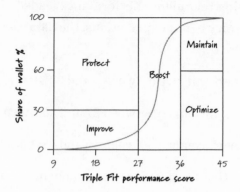

The Five Strategic Moves

As mentioned, our consortia research with more than a hundred companies has identified five possible strategic moves emerging from the S-curve relationship between Triple Fit performance and share of wallet based on the position of the relationships on the booster zone grid. Each of these five strategic moves improves a business relationship through value-cocreation focus with the customer. Next, we describe each of these in more detail with case examples from participating companies that we advised on relationship breakthroughs during the consortia.

1. Strategic move "improve"

The strategic move "improve" is characterized by a need to improve the Triple Fit performance by primarily addressing the capabilities that ranked the lowest during the Triple Fit performance rating assessment. This kind of a relationship indicates a need to allocate resources to improve the Triple Fit performance and move the relationship into the S-curve zone, where the share of wallet can benefit from a rise or boost in growth. This strategic move is highlighted

FIGURE 4-6

Strategic move "improve"—Thermo Fisher Scientific and Instituto Biológico

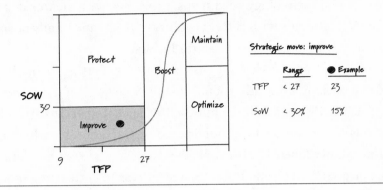

graphically in figure 4-6 with the example of US-based firm Thermo Fisher Scientific (supplier) and Brazilian-based Instituto Biológico (customer).

Thermo Fisher Scientific, a world leader in scientific instruments, equipment, software, services, and consumables, focuses on developing a high-value relationship with one of its top strategic customers, Instituto Biológico, an applied research center organized in 1924 in São Paulo, Brazil. The latter is a governmental organization concerned with the prevention of zoonoses and foodborne animal pathogens such as rabies and tuberculosis, sanitary advertisement campaigns, and alternatives to the chemical control of diseases such as organic farming and biological control. Instituto Biológico is a strategic customer for Thermo Fisher Scientific, and with its positioning in the improve zone, it is ready for growth on the foundation of strong multilevel contacts.

An initial Triple Fit assessment showed strength in the areas of strategies, which were starting to see joint planning of strategic initiatives; relationships, with empowered contact persons on both sides; structures, with strong cross-functional collaboration; and knowledge, where continuous best practices and knowledge sharing were starting to take shape as well. However, there was clear need for improvement in communications with multilevel communications and sharing of forecasts, solutions with need for joint development of programs and technology road maps, processes with clearer definition of roles, systems with better visibility of stock, and finally people, with teams that could act as trusted advisers.

Starting out as a divisional customer for agribusiness, Instituto Biológico became a multidivisional customer because of the relationship Thermo Fisher Scientific built with the customer. Instituto Biológico is a complex and multidivisional organization for which the Thermo Fisher Scientific team needed to develop a closer relationship. The goal for Thermo Fisher Scientific was to better understand the strategy of Instituto Biológico, so the team presented the Triple Fit canvas and the results to the former division it had worked with. That division then arranged a meeting with top management. The Thermo Fisher Scientific team again presented the Triple Fit canvas and learned from the customer team members what their major strategies were and got the go-ahead to talk to them and suggest solutions.

With a goal to improve the relationship across multiple levels, Thermo Fisher Scientific is continuing to grow with Instituto Biológico. A critical strategic element was the involvement of the customer's top management teams, for which the Triple Fit canvas was not only an icebreaker but a discussion basis, leading to many valuable insights across different business dimensions.

The relationship with Instituto Biológico demonstrates what our research shares about value cocreation. It really makes a difference if your customer relationships are managed by network-oriented managers and their teams that have the skills and competence to not only orchestrate multilevel contacts with the customers but keep their trust. We call this the "orchestrator perspective," which leads to greater value creation within the wider supplier-customer ecosystem; we will further elaborate in chapter 7. These contacts not only to the executive teams but across different levels of a complex organization are the foundation for accessing valuable information, including the customer's strategy, needs across solutions, processes, and systems, as well as the knowledge that accelerates joint development programs. Thermo Fisher Scientific has taken the relationship with Instituto Biológico in the right direction by opening the right dialogues and creating mutual trust with the customer. Strong relationships will continue to be an important part of Thermo Fisher Scientific's journey with Instituto Biológico, creating greater success in the long term.

2. Strategic move "protect"

The strategic move "protect" is characterized by a need to protect the share of wallet, which is high despite a low Triple Fit performance. This kind of a relationship indicates a transactional or price-based focus. This is the most precarious position in the graph, as there is constant external threat to the revenue. There is a need to establish better dialogue with the customer as a starting point for relationship improvement and allocation of resources toward collaboration efforts. If the customer is both high volume and strategically important, relationship improvement efforts are a must to not only protect the share of wallet but to protect the relationship itself. This strategic move is presented in figure 4-7 based on the example of VAT (supplier) and Magnum (customer).

FIGURE 4-7

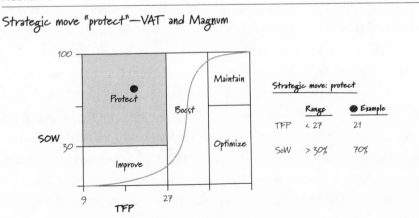

Strategic move "protect"—VAT and Magnum

VAT Vakuumventile AG, a leading supplier for vacuum valves and related services in the semiconductor, display, and solar sectors, is headquartered in Haag, Switzerland. A high-potential customer of VAT that we call Magnum already had a high share of wallet. Yet, there was a lot of untapped potential, specifically on relationships and knowledge-sharing. Through the Triple Fit performance assessment, VAT found that the overall relationship with the customer was far from where it could be. The relationship needed to be protected and maintained, at the risk of losing the share of wallet. A key area of concern for VAT was that even though the customer was active in the same markets as VAT, there was nearly no strategic and personal exchange at the senior level. This had been much neglected in the past, albeit an obvious customer desire.

The relationship between VAT and Magnum indicated an opportunity for mutual understanding of not only their respective product strategies, but the larger market environment context in which they operated. There was a clear overlap in the industry and market areas of the two firms, thus creating a need for interfirm interactions that permit the transfer, recombination, or creation of specialized knowledge, through the institutionalized interfirm processes purposefully designed to facilitate knowledge exchanges between two firms.

VAT realized that some key actions would enhance the relationship significantly. As a first and important step, it needed to establish a regular executive exchange. This improved the leadership unity and returned strategic alignment and access to confidential, otherwise unshared information. Executive relationships also created much-needed strategic impact such as supporting Magnum in its business in Asia.

Moreover, as the customer was active globally with multiple independent subsidiaries, a regular account review among all involved sales team members improved their understanding of the customer and its market environment. Further, to enhance knowledge sharing, a joint summit between the two companies helped them to identify possible mutual approaches to new markets and applications, as both companies had an excellent network worldwide to profit from.

With these steps, VAT was able to recognize and value the external knowledge coming from its partner, Magnum, and to combine it with internal knowledge to develop new products or strategies. By establishing better dialogue with the customer along with multilevel networking, VAT found the right starting point for relationship improvement. With this, it was able to not only protect the relationship but also help it transition to its growth potential.

3. Strategic move "boost"

The strategic move "boost" is characterized by a need to let the relationship benefit from a placement on the S-curve leading to a sharp rise or a boost in the share of wallet. This is the most advantageous position in the graph. This kind of a relationship is ready to take off in the right direction with collaboration efforts and resource commitments capitalizing on existing opportunities and areas of strength with the customer and addressing the capabilities that need attention. This strategic move is highlighted in figure 4-8 with the case of Schaerer (supplier) and Magnolia (customer).

Three years earlier, Schaerer, a leading Swiss manufacturer specializing in coffee machines for the hotel and catering industry, faced

FIGURE 4-8

Strategic move "boost"—Schaerer and Magnolia

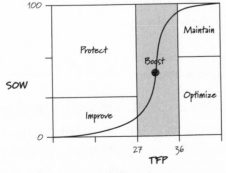
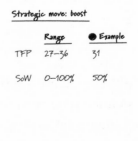

competition for its customer business an international chain of convenience stores headquartered in the United States that we call Magnolia. Because Schaerer offerings met US product requirements, the firm had strong positioning in the market. However, there were several challenges due to high requirements and customer expectations, such as for product features including digital innovations, financing options, services, and agreements. On the Schaerer side, executive sponsors were represented up to the COO level, but not the CEO. The Triple Fit performance assessment between Schaerer and Magnolia showed that despite the challenges, there was a strong foundation in place for a boost strategy with existing strengths in strategies, relationships, and communication, combined with high-quality offerings from Schaerer and a strong customer-facing team on board.

The targeted growth with Magnolia was achieved stepwise through establishing networks both locally and globally. Schaerer built on its replacement planning and guided its innovation teams to continue developing winning solution offerings as key steps in the current scenario. First, a rollout was launched in the United States and secondly in Europe. In a third phase, Schaerer was planning to enter additional markets to grow further with Magnolia. Despite the competitive coffee-machines market, customer-centric innovation beyond products enabled by strong networks has been the key to achieving the intended growth. Furthermore, top management support has been a critical factor in its success. To conclude, the relationship with Magnolia demonstrates that innovation is about much more than new products and requires a focus on commercial processes and structures to give the relationship the boost it needs.

4. Strategic move "optimize"

The strategic move "optimize" is characterized by a need to address untapped share-of-revenue potential, because despite a high-performing relationship with a high Triple Fit performance, the share of wallet is still low. This kind of a relationship indicates the need to optimize relationship efforts that are missing the mark. There is a need to cut back on resource commitments that are not delivering results with the customer. If the customer business is high volume and strategically important, a higher share of wallet is long overdue. This strategic move is highlighted in figure 4-9 with the case of Maersk and Velocity.

Three years ago, Maersk faced several challenges for the business with its customer that we will call Velocity amid great uncertainty and a change of key people associated with the account. Velocity is a leading multinational corporation that designs and manufactures athletic and casual footwear, apparel, and accessories.

The relationship with Velocity was already at a strategic level, reflecting high relationship performance and indicating a joint collaborative focus. However, there was need for greater strategic focus and efforts, including at the C-level. Maersk knew that it could not underestimate the role of its executive sponsors, as top management involvement in customer relationships can pay enormous dividends and the most positive relationships demonstrate high relationship building and high revenue seeking—or what we call the growth champion executive role and will elaborate on in chapter 8. Maersk needed to cultivate these growth champions.

FIGURE 4-9

Strategic move "optimize"—Maersk and Velocity

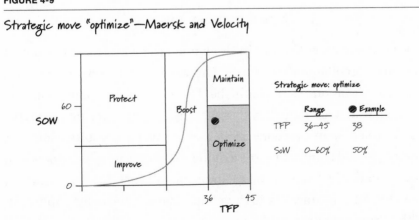

The management was able to make several important and much-needed decisions for the account, such as a sustainable approach and a better structure across the different business units, enabling a growth track with the customer. The growth champions identified for Velocity achieved a greater collaborative focus through understanding the customer's strategic thinking, literally stepping into the shoes of the customer. The relationships between key stakeholders improved and became stronger compared to the competition. Maersk became perceived as a partner that could deliver many current solutions but was also innovative. Maersk's global account setup came on the right track, with frequent C-level interactions. The communication with the customer stayed proactive, especially in the current global scenario, and operational procedures focused on finding efficiencies and on cost reductions.

This created an overall positive position with the customer and took the account in a growth direction. The Maersk team has been able to ensure that its partnership is strategic, putting it in an excellent spot for further planning and execution. Despite the competitive retail market, Maersk's customer-centric strategic actions have been the key to achieving a high relationship performance with Velocity and continuing to grow the share of wallet. This was truly a benchmark example of creatively reinforcing the high-value relationship between the two companies.

5. Strategic move "maintáin"

The strategic move "maintain" is characterized by a need to support the existing collaboration efforts. This kind of a relationship indicates an ideal situation where both the Triple Fit performance and the share of wallet are high. It shows that the existing offerings, resource commitments, and revenue model are delivering results. However, there is a need to maintain the driving speed or cruising altitude with the customer by keeping the relationship efforts steady, especially if the customer business is high volume and strategically important. This strategic move is highlighted in figure 4-10 with the example of Evonik and Dragon Food.

FIGURE 4-10

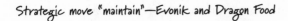

Strategic move "maintain"—Evonik and Dragon Food

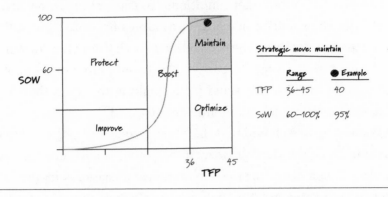

When we were engaged with Evonik, the German-based specialty chemicals manufacturer, to evaluate its business with the top three hundred customers, we found that the relationship with its Asian-based customer Dragon Food was already in very good shape. Dragon Food is a producer of feed, shrimp, poultry, and pork. Both booster zone indicators, the share of wallet and the Triple Fit performance, showed significantly higher results than many other relationships. At the same time, the global economy and business outlooks were not looking favorable. Evonik questioned whether it could maintain the high position given the constraints of further economy shocks. But thanks to the well-established Triple Fit principles, both companies were able to cut through the turmoil of the crisis. Looking at the macro data from both market development teams, the management teams decided to hold firm to the initial plans to build a new, global-scale plant for producing methionine, an amino acid used in livestock production to feed animals healthily, efficiently, and sustainably.

Understanding that the world market would still need more food production capacity, both companies decided to locate the plant strategically on Jurong Island in Singapore, despite the financial crisis. With an investment of more than €1 billion, the plant went live in two phases.[9] Thanks to the existing alignment at the planning fit level,

Dragon Food and Evonik established not only the trust but also the transparency for engaging in such large-scale projects ahead of time and despite difficult market conditions. To support the heavy investment from the supplier side at the resources fit level, Dragon Food agreed to take almost all the production capacity from the start of the plant's operational time. In early 2023, Evonik announced another expansion of the Jurong Island plant, making the plant the largest production complex for methionine in the world.[10]

To sum up, we've found that the booster zone grid is the key to not only unlocking the right growth strategy but also overcoming resistance and so on. Knowing in which zone your relationships are helps identify joint value-creation potential to produce synergies for both companies that are joining forces. It is also important to manage the collaboration effectively and ensure that the right growth strategy comes into play, given the joint capabilities of both businesses.

In the next chapter, we will see how to take the strategic moves to the next level of customer-validated growth by focusing on a key ingredient of the booster zone grid success: improvement of the Triple Fit performance, and how to do this consistently in quarterly intervals, especially when the odds are against you.

TAKEAWAYS

- The three Triple Fit principles for growth are: (1) realign your planning; (2) reconfigure your execution; and (3) reallocate your resources.

- There is an S-curve relationship between Triple Fit performance (sum of all nine ratings) and share of wallet (accessible customer spend).

- Based on the position of the relationships on the booster zone grid, there are five possible strategic moves: improve, protect, boost, optimize, and maintain.

REFLECTION QUESTIONS

- If you plot your top customers on the booster zone grid, how does the picture look based on the estimated Triple Fit performance and share of wallet?

- How many of these customers are in the booster zone? What actions could you take to boost growth for these customers?

- How would validated customer ratings and Triple Fit performance change the picture? Go to triplefitstrategy.com to download a free booster zone grid.

CHAPTER 5

EXECUTE VALIDATED GROWTH PLANS

In early 2020, when Covid-19 was still under the early mysterious fog of rare occurrences and undetected cases, Josefina Godoy Lemos was one of the account managers for Hillebrand-Gori (now a DHL company) attending one of our training programs. A cornerstone of this training was for each participant to develop a real-life value creation project. In her case, she focused on new growth opportunities with her strategic customer, Grupo Peñaflor, one of the largest wine producers in Argentina and one of the ten largest in the world.[1] She believed that conducting a Triple Fit analysis of her company's work with Peñaflor would determine where to improve the relationship. She also wanted to identify areas where Hillebrand could cut into Peñaflor's relationship with one of Hillebrand's competitors. Defining new value propositions for Peñaflor seemed to be an uphill battle, and Lemos needed a game-changer strategy with Peñaflor.

The pandemic drove up orders for Peñaflor. Key markets such as the United States, the UK, and the Netherlands grew by 30 percent in the first six months of 2020. Hillebrand needed to respond to the demand quickly, loading wines from its Buenos Aires or Chilean ports and sending them out across the world. The upcoming winter season (from May to September in the southern hemisphere) could interrupt the international roads connecting Mendoza to Chilean ports with snowstorms, increasing the total lead time for wine delivery by three or four weeks. Lemos needed to find a cost-effective solution, and fast.

In Lemos's case, when Hillebrand and Peñaflor filled out a Triple Fit canvas together through the process described in chapter 2, the customer-validated ratings with Peñaflor revealed that as partners, they struggled with several Triple Fit components, most notably strategies, processes, and systems (see figure 5-1). The Triple Fit performance score was at twenty-seven points, and the estimated share of wallet at 30 percent, just at the edge between the improve and boost

FIGURE 5-1

Triple Fit performance and booster zone grid for Hillebrand and Peñaflor

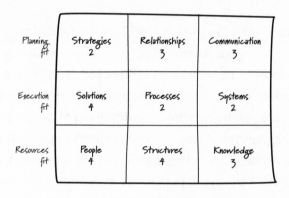

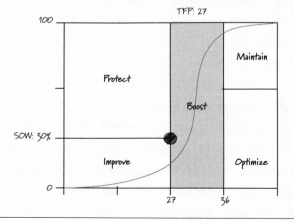

zones. If Lemos could identify the growth drivers and priorities from a customer perspective, there was a huge growth potential waiting to be captured. A root cause analysis based on step two of the Triple Fit process (asking why for each of the nine building blocks) revealed that improving the execution fit for Peñaflor was paramount for Hillebrand to successfully meet the customer's requirements. Strategy sharing between the two companies also needed to improve to enable a better understanding between stakeholders from both Hillebrand and Peñaflor. This is where Hillebrand needed a clear growth plan with Peñaflor that was not just a usual account plan.

Transforming Account Plans into Growth Plans

In chapter 1, we saw that customer-centricity is the foundation for growth. In chapter 2, we saw how the Triple Fit canvas is a tool for capturing each stage of the strategic dialogue in the five steps in a tangible manner. In chapter 3, we saw how game-changers emerge from these five steps and how we can take them to the next level. In chapter 4, we learned about the booster zone grid with five strategic moves based on the existing Triple Fit performance that help identify the growth potential for any given customer. This chapter ties much of the work in those previous chapters together through what we call a Triple Fit growth plan that transforms the analytical inputs from the Triple Fit canvas and the booster zone grid into a solid, customer-validated growth plan.

Sales techniques aside, more than ever, today's B2B sellers are expected to plan and document their activities in a transparent way.[2] This can happen in the form of a customer relationship management (CRM) log, a sales call report, or—what we most often encounter—the so-called account plan (sometimes called a client development plan, customer strategy, or something similar). The average account plan consists of dozens of PowerPoint slides documenting sales history, a competitive landscape, and a future sales pipeline. When it comes to strategy, however, the content is often alarmingly thin.

One of the biggest obstacles to growth with customers is that often these cross-region, cross-business unit accounts are managed by their account teams through the shared account plans stored in CRM systems.[3] But with very, very few exceptions, we've seen that most of these account plans follow the logic of product selling instead of value creation. While account plans have their place in the management of these strategic customers, they are limited when it comes to creating breakthrough growth through a strategic dialogue with customers.[4]

If the business year is set from January to December, early autumn is one of the most hated periods for many B2B sales organizations, when account managers are revisiting the account plan templates they're required to submit to their leaders. Over several weeks, they fill dozens of CRM templates and spreadsheets. And we all know the questions running through their heads: What did we write a year ago? What is this year's new template format? And how long will it take to fill out the forms nobody is going to read anyway? Finally, the account plans are updated—some better, some worse—and sales leaders happily tick the box in the corresponding performance indicator section. The organization then returns to business as usual for the next twelve months, before the same procedure happens again.

One year later, everybody wonders why the plans did not yield the intended results. Of course, there will be positive exceptions, more like pleasant surprises. But for most sales organizations we have observed in the past two decades, the account plans do not yield the desired outcomes. The reason: they are wish lists, lacking a customer-validated strategy.

In fact, after reviewing hundreds of these sales documents, we can confirm that the top three shortcomings of these documents were the following:

- No customer validation

- No standard format

- No internal mandate

But there is more trouble ahead. Our client work confirms that over 90 percent of sales teams do not share these account plans with customers.[5] The reasons for not sharing them are reasonably consistent:

- We are not allowed to share our plan.

- The customer is not interested or will disclose the information to the competition.

- We don't have a good story to tell.

If companies do not change their perspectives, most of these issues will either remain or even further intensify. The solution is to manage a strategic customer by having a clear and validated growth plan with it.[6]

How can companies do that? It all starts with acknowledging that account planning is not bad per se. But most account plan templates are wrongly designed, especially those in the well-known CRM systems. These plans focus mainly on the analysis part with aspects like sales history and forecasts, relationship and power maps, opportunity pipelines, followed by an action section with some call and meeting activities popping up in the calendars of the CRM users. What's missing is the *strategy* part, which in turn creates two problems. First, adding a strategy section requires more profound thinking than just jumping from internal analysis to internal action planning. Classic account plans often feel like planning by looking into the rearview mirror. And second, the strategy needs to be battle-proof; in business terms, it must be customer-validated. And that is where the Triple Fit canvas comes into play. It does not eliminate the need for account plans, but it adds the necessary *external validation* element.

Our research has shown that many account plans (more than 80 percent) consist of only two of the three components of a growth plan. While analysis and actions exist and are captured well in the CRM systems—for example, via executed sales orders of the past, projections of the future deal pipeline, or daily action lists in the calendar—the strategy part is usually alarmingly thin or nonexistent.[7]

Taken to a higher level, the same problem exists when you look at company strategy. Strategy author and former dean of the Rotman School of Management, Roger L. Martin, once said, "The vast majority of strategic plans that I have seen over 30 years of working in the strategy realm are simply budgets with lots of explanatory words attached."[8] This is exactly the problem with account plans as well. If a strategy section exists, it usually consists of sales goals—a statement like "Our strategy is to become the preferred supplier." Of course, that's not a strategy; it's an ambition. But imagine a world where account plans are turbocharged by customer-validated Triple Fit canvases. The consequences would be dramatic, because for the first time, companies could also justify their strategy based on the validated plans with their top customers.

We are not advocating a costly change or upgrade of CRM systems or a time-consuming makeover of account plan templates. All we are proposing is a new way of looking at account plans and making them more real. In turn, this will draw the attention of both supplier and customer management and generate the required resources to make the plan work. So adding a Triple Fit canvas that the customer continuously validates is a real game-changer in itself.

Most account plans are wish lists, because they are not customer-validated. But it's equally important for suppliers to keep sensitive information such as final profitability figures and so on confidential. So, sharing CRM access or the screen with customers is mostly neither feasible nor legally allowed. In the ideal planning sequence "analysis–strategy–action," the Triple Fit canvas can help address the missing link, solving this predicament. Hence, as a new way of looking at customer relationships, adding the Triple Fit canvas as the strategy part to the account plan is a great opportunity to engage with the customer in a strategic dialogue via a one-page document that is constantly kept up to date together with the customer. In the next section, we take a closer look at how to incorporate Triple Fit into a growth plan.

Incorporating Triple Fit into Growth Plans

A Triple Fit–powered growth plan ensures that companies maintain their persistence in customer-centric initiatives and internal change efforts through clear planning, focused execution, and well-defined resource allocation. It maps out a feasible plan to achieve the goals that are identified through the five steps of the Triple Fit process and through the booster zone grid, which clarifies the strategic move that is relevant to any given business relationship. As we just saw, a complete account planning sequence has three components: analysis, strategy, and actions. Consequently, an ideal account plan has three sections building on these three components. We can incorporate key insights from the Triple Fit canvas in each of the three resulting sections.

With the Triple Fit included, the analysis section focuses on the current state of customer engagement and answers the following questions:

- How is this relationship performing across the nine Triple Fit building blocks and what are the customer's priorities?

- What kind of insights (strategic options) are emerging from the booster zone analysis?

The strategy section focuses on the strategic plan for unlocking growth and answers the following questions:

- What compelling Triple Fit story (aka the business case for change) and key asks are emerging from the analysis?

- What is the anticipated delta that the jointly validated game-changer idea will deliver?

And finally, the actions section focuses on the road to get there—the implementation plan—and answers the following questions:

- What will it take to bring the road map to reality and how can my executive sponsor help?

- What could kill the approach and how do you mitigate this risk?

FIGURE 5-2

Components of a Triple Fit growth plan

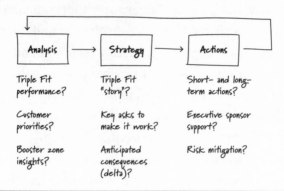

In the case of Hillebrand and Peñaflor, what did Josefina Lemos do to make it work? She needed to overcome the limitations of an inside-out focused account plan that was not validated by the customer. She also knew that she couldn't simply walk into a meeting with Hillebrand leaders and tell them that she wanted to create growth based on the initial Triple Fit analysis she had done with Peñaflor. Only after developing a clear understanding of who would be involved, when, and how the actions would unfold, would she be able to persuade her leadership team to support her initiatives. So, she developed a Triple Fit growth plan together with her customer.

For Lemos, the growth plan was focused on finding inventory solutions for Peñaflor critical to the customer's strategy. It was not just about securing cross-docking space for Peñaflor's orders at Hillebrand's warehouse but taking the necessary legal and security measures as well as visibility and control systems with IT global team support. Offering warehousing solutions in Chile catering to the Covid-19 demand urgency for loading the wines (pallets or cases) close to the port, instead of at the customer's facility in Mendoza, was one such perfect move.[9] The Hillebrand team began engaging with the customer at a value-creation level by getting a clear understanding of the various stakeholders and operations. A detailed cost analysis showed they could cut costs by cutting lead times and inventory and making small but significant improvements across the nine Triple Fit building blocks.

These insights led Lemos to identify the activities needed to implement the insights she had discovered in the previous steps. She implemented her growth plan in the following sequence:

- Analysis: With her Peñaflor counterparts, Lemos captured opportunities in potential areas for improvement.

- Strategy: The most important factor was garnering the support of teams on both sides to make the proposed cost-saving ideas a reality.

- Actions: With time and money being critical factors, Lemos identified the ninety-day quick wins that required less effort and could be implemented right away and the long-term plans that would take more time.

The sales team led by Lemos acting as an orchestrator helped Hillebrand to identify $7.8 million of additional revenue, reduce lead times, save significant truck delay hours, and decrease CO_2 emissions. At the same time, the initiative reduced Peñaflor's logistics costs significantly, and Hillebrand-Gori continued to increase its revenue and profitability, and was thus able to create significant value for its customer with its focus and purposeful direction.

Executing Validated Growth Plans

When it comes to the customer portfolio, for most B2B companies, the 80-20 rule applies.[10] So-called key accounts, about 20 percent of all accounts, represent up to 80 (or even more) percent of revenue and margin. This strategy comes with its pros and cons. It does create immense potential for mutually defined growth. But it also means that losing business with one strategic customer can have a devastating long-term effect on a company's growth.[11] This is where mutual growth based on the value-creation perspective of Triple Fit rather than a transactional approach becomes increasingly critical. Over the last two decades, we have observed that Triple Fit growth plans are to value creation what account plans are to product selling. The latter, as we have just observed, are still a one-way street, where the most critical element of the plan—the customer—is left out of the planning. In the following sections, we share three best practices that enable the execution of customer-validated growth plans.

Defining growth areas together with customers

When d&b audiotechnik, a German manufacturer of professional sound systems, wanted to incorporate customer inputs in its account plans, it faced the exact same challenges. Its products and services are used around the globe by top acts in the music industry such as The Who, Madonna, Lady Gaga, Coldplay, Taylor Swift, and many more. In early 2023, when we were working with Ralf Koehler, d&b audiotechnik's head of global business, he was facing the challenge to expand the business into the high-end restaurant market. He used the Triple Fit canvas to create the customer-validated game-changer idea and complement his formerly inward-looking account plans with an external view on what's necessary to create mutual growth with customers. Targeting Azumi Group, an award-winning global restaurant business based in London and a d&b audiotechnik customer, he learned that, not surprisingly, the quality of the technical solutions his company provided was rated very high. People and communication got high ratings, too. But strategies, systems, and knowledge received very low ratings. It would take focused efforts in these three building blocks to support the anticipated transition from a pure vendor role into a strategic partner position (see figure 5-3).

Based on the three focus areas for further improvement, Koehler built stepwise, in close collaboration with Azumi, a growth plan to create more value for the customer. This included, for example, the

FIGURE 5-3

Initial Triple Fit ratings for d&b audiotechnik and Azumi Group

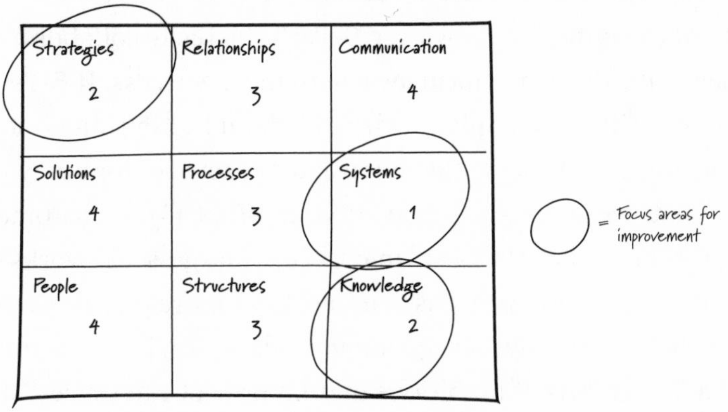

Strategies	Relationships	Communication
2	3	4
Solutions	Processes	Systems
4	3	1
People	Structures	Knowledge
4	3	2

= Focus areas for improvement

setup of a new business line for mobile outdoor equipment that further increased total customer experience and additional value elements, focusing on systems and knowledge. Six months later, the situation had significantly improved, and d&b audiotechnik is now managing Azumi's project pipeline from New York and Las Vegas to Dubai and Bangkok, without making costly tender offers. On top of that, d&b audiotechnik has also started to replicate its value-creation approach with cruise ship companies such as Aida, P&O, and Disney, all offering new and profitable business beyond mere product sales.

Triple Fit workshops versus Triple Fit interviews

In order to further ensure that the customer inputs are included in the growth plans, we strongly recommend entering the strategic dialogue in the same way as in all the examples in this chapter. One way of doing this is to run Triple Fit workshops. However, the conversations may sometimes yield unexpected results, as in the case of what we call B-Tech, a global supplier of building technology shows. After a half-day Triple Fit workshop, B-Tech learned that partnering with Swedish furniture maker IKEA at a global level was not a priority because of IKEA's preferred strategy for purchasing locally, and, hence, would not deliver the anticipated value. Thus, the supplier company reallocated expensive global sales resources for other, more suitable customers. At the same time, however, B-Tech started to collaborate more intensely with IKEA at a local level with much success. If B-Tech had only followed its account plan with analysis and action but no strategy elements in its CRM, it would have wasted resources for many years.

But what if the odds are against you? What if the customer just tells you that it's not the best time to run a large-scale workshop or engage in deep strategy discussions, as it has more pressing issues to solve? What if not only the economy heads south, but also you are a newcomer with lots of ambitions and no project references? This is exactly the story of Cilcare, a French biotech startup that was using classic account plans to attract new business. For more than eighteen months, it found little success. The breakthrough came when Cilcare's CEO, Celia Belline, decided to use the Triple Fit canvas to qualify new opportunities in more depth. After we coached her team to run thirty- to sixty-minute Triple Fit interviews with prospect contacts, the company learned more about the priorities of potential customers than ever before. Framing the Triple Fit conversation in a startup way, the ten questions (see chapter 2) did not serve as a basis for a Triple Fit rating, but more as a basis for minimum conditions to consider for a pilot project. Consequently, Cilcare decided to focus resources on jointly identified pilot projects. Twelve months later, the company had doubled its sales with one of its top customers and won several new projects with target accounts that turned into active customers.

As the above examples have shown, executing validated growth plans starts with customer validation of the Triple Fit canvas inputs. The validation can be accomplished via either a Triple Fit workshop scheduled up front or a series of interviews with a final workshop (if possible). The experience of the Covid-19 pandemic has also shown that the format can (and will) vary due to safety and health requirements.[12] Figure 5-4 compares the two formats and illustrates under

FIGURE 5-4

Triple Fit workshops versus Triple Fit interviews—when they work best

	Workshop	Interview
Triple Fit performance	Low	High
Share of wallet	High	Low
Availability of key stakeholders	High	Low
Willingness to collaborate	High	Low
Competition	High	Low
Time pressure/urgency	High	Low
Geographic scope	Local/Regional	Global/Regional

which conditions they work best. For example, when the availability of key stakeholders is high, a workshop is ideal. On the other hand, when the willingness to collaborate is low, individual interviews are better.

A caveat: we are not advocating that one format is better than another. In many cases, we have seen a combined approach work best, first starting with a few quick interviews with key stakeholders from the customer side for thirty minutes to get a first impression. As already described in chapter 2, the checklist with the ten initial questions works well as a blueprint for the interview. You can also use it as a basis and preparation for the workshops by sending the ten questions to workshop participants a few days in advance. These are usually the key counterparts on the customer and supplier sides representing a few different functions and, in an ideal scenario, include the members of the senior leadership teams on both sides. Our experience has shown that this provides sufficient insights to enter the Triple Fit process with the why-what-how interpretation sequence.

During the pandemic, we also observed a variation of the workshop format born out of the sheer necessity to adapt to virtual communication channels.[13] Acknowledging that the energy and attention levels over a full day is hard to maintain in the virtual setup, many of the Triple Fit users we coached switched to shorter sessions.

An often-observed example was to split an initially scheduled in-person workshop of one full day into three sessions of two to three hours spread over two weeks. This approach worked especially well in international contexts. What was refreshing to see was that after the pandemic, these teams still gathered in person to further strengthen the initially built personal ties.

Pitching your growth plan with the Triple Fit story

Executing a successfully developed and validated Triple Fit growth plan also requires regular pitching to your stakeholders via a so-called Triple Fit story. A compelling Triple Fit story consists of three elements:

- A crisp central message that can be understood in ten seconds

- Three key asks for decisions or further-support requests that are beyond your span of control

- A crystal-clear summary of what will most likely happen if the pitch is approved or not

As we showed in the sequence of "analysis–strategy–action," the Triple Fit canvas is the missing link to customer-validated plans. To validate these plans, you need to embed them into a compelling story. The three components of a Triple Fit story are a central message, up to three key asks resulting from the Triple Fit canvas process sequence (Why? What? How?), and the anticipated financial consequences if the pitch is approved or not approved. Figure 5-5 provides a closer look at the link between Triple Fit canvas and Triple Fit story.

The following checklist helps you to present your Triple Fit story in the most compelling way, embedded in the business context of the selected relationship. Usually, the pitch includes key financials of the past, present, and future. The recommended five presentation steps represent the experiences from hundreds of successfully delivered pitches and consist of an easy-to-learn flow. Your goal is to achieve buy-in from your stakeholder(s) in less than ten minutes.[14]

FIGURE 5-5

The link between Triple Fit canvas and Triple Fit story

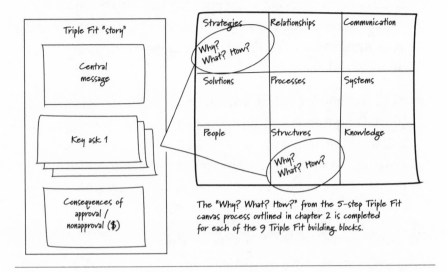

The "Why? What? How?" from the 5-step Triple Fit canvas process outlined in chapter 2 is completed for each of the 9 Triple Fit building blocks.

1. First, deliver the central message. Then present an overview of the overall situation. Summarize the strengths and weaknesses of your business relationship. Be brief and focus on the Triple Fit canvas building blocks with the highest and lowest ratings. Ideally, all business partners have already validated these results.

2. Second, turn to the financial part of the relationship and briefly summarize the past, the present, and the anticipated future status. Keep in mind that your chances to win approval for your case will significantly increase if you label the consolidated three-year revenue stream of the future as the business at stake.

3. Third, tell your audience again what this relationship is all about. Phrase the central message in a way that it catches the attention of the audience immediately. You may want to think of it as a news headline or a movie title that creates a sense of urgency. Then talk about the supporting facts and repeat the central message before you move on to the next step.

4. Fourth, break down your decision proposals, investment, and support requests in a maximum number of three key asks. Keep in mind that a key ask is not a key task. Tasks are actions you can start and end all by yourself. Asks, however, go beyond your authority and require high-level approval or buy-in from multiple stakeholders.

5. Fifth, summarize the consequences of the key ask being approved or not approved. Clearly emphasize the expected results and what the involved parties will get in more detail if your proposed approach is endorsed by your stakeholder(s). Also point out negative consequences of nonapproval (i.e., status quo, loss of business, etc.).

The work on the Triple Fit story never stops, and a central message pitch is only relevant for a certain period. Circling back to the Maersk-Kotahi example, the winning central message that was presented in 2022 to the stakeholders read as follows: "Joining capabilities and integrating eco-systems to enable New Zealand businesses to win on the global stage." (To illustrate the context, we present the outcome of the discussion in figure 5-6.)

Next, we present two additional examples of central messages that evolved nicely over several rounds of discussions that we facilitated. The first example is the case of a supplier to Italian-based aerospace,

FIGURE 5-6

Maersk's Triple Fit story pitch to Kotahi

FIGURE 5-7

First and second pitch drafts to Leonardo Helicopters

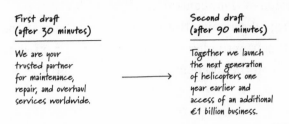

defense, and security group Leonardo (see figure 5-7). Calling on Leonardo's helicopter division, the supplier team came up with a first version, which purely focused on its own success. In an internal test pitch, it realized that flipping the perspective to the customer's point of view would yield the same results but create a much stronger buy-in at all levels. Consequently, the second version was much more customer-focused and resonated well with the customer team.

The second example describes the case of an IT supplier to Swiss Re, a leading reinsurer, with headquarters in Zurich, Switzerland (see figure 5-8). The supplier team was tasked to come up with a central message to convince stakeholders that they were the most capable partner for Swiss Re's transition to a fully cloud-based organization. While the first pitch version was all about the IT-supplier team's ambition, the second pitch version was addressing the heart of Swiss Re's mission as a company.

FIGURE 5-8

First and second pitch drafts to Swiss Re

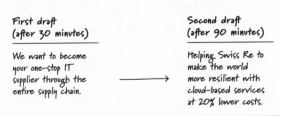

The bottom line is that developing and executing validated growth plans is doable, and so is pitching. All these companies prepared a revised version of their central message in thirty minutes. They also benefited from developing this together with their customers, hence, validating the growth plan in real time. In the next chapter, we will see how to keep the momentum going once a growth plan has been put in place.

TAKEAWAYS

- A validated growth plan consists of three components: analysis, strategy, and actions. In most account plans, Triple Fit can (and will) complement the strategy section.

- First-time growth plan validation should not take longer than three months. If the odds are against you and no workshop is possible, start with Triple Fit interviews.

- A solid growth plan includes a Triple Fit story pitch building on a central message, up to three key asks, and the consequences of approval or nonapproval.

REFLECTION QUESTIONS

- What is the structure of your account plan documents?

- How could your account plan benefit from a customer-validated Triple Fit canvas? Go to triplefitstrategy.com for further guidance.

- Which method would fast-track your growth plan validation with customers: Triple Fit workshops or interviews?

CHAPTER 6

KEEP THE GROWTH MOMENTUM

In the early part of this decade, a global car manufacturer that we call Worldcar announced that it was pivoting to become a "mobility company." While it is still an evolving buzz phrase in the automobile industry, it meant that although Worldcar made and sold cars, it was also going to make those cars into rolling data collectors and earn value from the data those cars generated, or in other words, it would digitalize its products—the cars. When Worldcar's partner Vodafone, a communications service provider, learned of this strategy, it saw a massive opportunity. The market size for this kind of data was estimated to be $739 billion by 2030.[1] Miro Milojkovic, the global account director for Worldcar at Vodafone, identified alignment with customer strategy as the breakthrough factor for growth. If Vodafone could align with Worldcar as a collaborative partner, it estimated that it could grow revenue by a factor of four.

For Milojkovic's team, the path to achieving this ambition was to incorporate the customer input into its existing account plan and identify the focus areas for collaboration through the Triple Fit canvas. It also meant understanding its current performance in these areas and the changes necessary to unlock new growth, thus making it critical for success with the customer. Using the Triple Fit, Vodafone strengthened its executive-level relationships and involved the executive sponsors to make sure they had the right factors in place for growth. The strategy with the customer was focused on bridging Worldcar's technology gap in this new playing field and quicker time to market, offering new services supporting safety, user experience, and cost reduction, creating a competitive advantage over competition, and supporting Worldcar's strategy.

After diligently working on this for two years throughout the Covid-19 pandemic, which hit the automobile industry hard, Vodafone began seeing results with its customer, including a greater alignment between their respective C-levels. This resulted in Worldcar being one of the few accounts that had a double digit year-on-year growth even in a challenging economic situation and also unlocking access to an additional multimillion in revenue for the supplier.

So how did Milojkovic successfully implement the growth strategy with Worldcar despite all the challenges and obstacles to growth? He ensured the momentum in three phases:

1. The first phase was about validating his growth plan ideas with his customer counterparts and securing his own company's commitment through executive sponsor support, focused on the Triple Fit building block "relationships."

2. The second phase was focused on creating pilot projects for the new digital services focused on the Triple Fit building blocks "processes" and "solutions."

3. The final phase was the commercial rollout of pilot projects in a step-by-step approach globally, focusing on the Triple Fit building blocks "strategies" and "structures." All these organizational factors enabled Vodafone's Triple Fit growth plans to become a reality.

Growth focused on value creation requires the organization to be ready for execution of the plans and to deal with the obstacles that may arise during implementation.[2] For example, if the right organizational structures or processes are not in place, it may become impossible to meet the new investment demands. Or the sales force may lack the skills needed to deal with the customer pain points or the organization itself may not be ready to handle the additional complexity that comes with growth.[3] Overcoming such (and many more) obstacles enables a company to focus on customer-centric initiatives and keep the growth momentum in place.

We have seen in our research that while it is one thing to have a growth plan in place, the successful cases also have another thing in common: they were able to keep momentum going in the face of the internal obstacles and external challenges, including unforeseen issues, organizational resistance, and many other demands that inevitably arise during a long implementation like a Triple Fit strategy. If companies cannot keep the momentum going, they are more likely to see good opportunities go by as people give up or fail to follow through.

In our consortium research with more than a hundred companies and analyzing more than ten thousand business relationships across industries and geographies, we have identified the most common momentum killers that hinder companies from keeping the growth momentum of their Triple Fit initiatives on track (see figure 6-1).

FIGURE 6-1

Momentum killers of growth in the nine Triple Fit building blocks

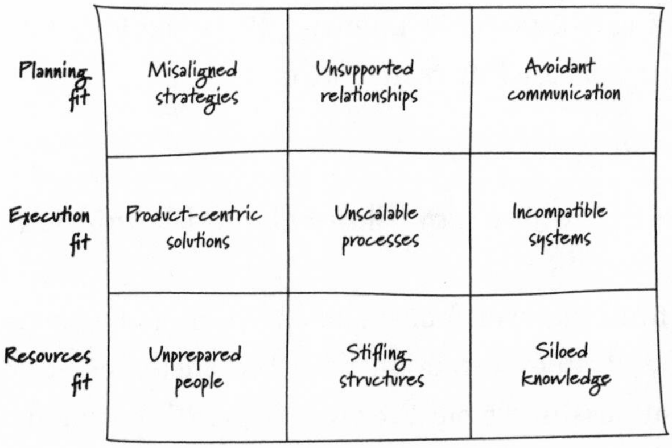

Planning fit	Misaligned strategies	Unsupported relationships	Avoidant communication
Execution fit	Product-centric solutions	Unscalable processes	Incompatible systems
Resources fit	Unprepared people	Stifling structures	Siloed knowledge

In total, we found the following nine momentum killers that can severely slow down or even kill your first successful Triple Fit activities:

1. Strategies: Neglected and misaligned strategic intentions

2. Relationships: Lack of executive sponsor support and growth champions

3. Communication: No strategic dialogue with the customer

4. Solutions: Product-centric thinking instead of a value cocreation mindset

5. Processes: Inefficiencies in processes while delivering the solutions

6. Systems: Inadequate IT, financial, and legal systems to collaborate with clients

7. People: Individuals and teams unprepared to focus on value creation

8. Structures: Organizational silos that hinder cross-functional alignment

9. Knowledge: Absence of knowledge sharing with the customer

As described in previous chapters, Triple Fit growth happens across three fit levels: planning, execution, and resources. Each of these levels presents its own momentum killers corresponding to the nine building blocks. In the following three sections, we will address the nine momentum killers in more detail.

Growth Momentum Killers at the Planning Fit Level

The planning fit level focuses on preparing the organization for setting the strategy direction with the customer at the planning stage. A successful Triple Fit growth plan implementation at this level requires: (1) bringing customer-validated strategic plans into

FIGURE 6-2

Three momentum killers of growth at the planning fit level

Planning fit

| Misaligned strategies | Unsupported relationships | Avoidant communication |

strategy discussions; (2) creating executive sponsor support for strategic customers; (3) making open, strategic communication with the customer an organizational best practice. There are three obstacles to overcome at this level, responding to the building blocks strategies, relationships, and communication (see figure 6-2).

Momentum killer 1: Misaligned strategies and how to overcome them

Corporate strategy often falls short of expectations when it comes to solving tangled issues involving many stakeholders, especially in an increasingly complex environment.[4] This happens mostly because the problems are often poorly structured as part of the corporate strategy process, if articulated at all.[5] The voice of customer-facing business units or frontline sales managers, who benefit from the advantage of directly collaborating with the customer as a part of their business activities, needs to be represented at the top management level.[6] Account plans are a key tool to achieve that, but we saw in the previous chapter how account plans are often not focused on strategy or do not have a value-creation perspective. A strategic, forward-looking plan not only captures the ongoing performance with the customer and the projected growth but includes the customer's strategic direction. Incorporating the inputs on customer strategy through forward-looking account plans not only provides knowledge of customer vision and strategy but helps identify the focus areas for collaboration. This is a valuable source of knowledge on where the customer firm is headed in the immediate future and helps identify new areas to unlock value with the customer.

When a global pharma supplier that we call Mercury began its transformational journey to customer-centricity, it realized that some key accounts did not perceive the company as a valued supplier or a strategic partner. They saw it simply as a device manufacturer and not a total solution provider, making its customer relationships more transactional in nature. Using the Triple Fit canvas to investigate the status of a handful of key account relationships in the pharmaceutical industry, Mercury learned that the situation was even worse than initially thought. In almost all cases, the strategic alignment was not even on the radar screen of both parties, leading to the transactional behavior and ongoing, frustrating price fights. Thus, misaligned strategies were a momentum killer of Mercury's growth with its strategic customers.

Taking the lessons from the Triple Fit initiative into account, Mercury aimed to rebuild its regional approach to a global one with the goal that its group entities be seen as "One Mercury." This involved not only leveraging its existing capabilities and defining an executive sponsor program but, more importantly, introducing a global lead at account level covering all Mercury entities and better support to the existing key account managers. The secret to overcoming the momentum killer of misaligned strategies was that the global lead function was tasked with aligning strategies internally *and* externally. For example, price differences in offers from different Mercury units were no longer tolerated. Or the global lead role intervened when local management wanted to raise prices to maximize local profits. The project doubled Mercury's sales and was a key step to enhancing and building stronger relationships with key global customers. Thus, the cross-organizational alignment function was critical for Mercury to establish a strategic and innovative partnership with its strategic customers and overcome the potential growth-momentum killer.

Momentum killer 2: Unsupported relationships and how to overcome them

The absence of an executive sponsor is highly detrimental to a business relationship, putting the supplier at a disadvantage versus its more active competitor that invests in executive sponsor coverage. Even the most dedicated customer-facing teams require executive sponsors to enable a strong, high-value relationship with the customer that often involves multiple contacts from the top level to the ground level, and various departments including operations and product teams.[7] The executive sponsor is a key interface between the two companies, orchestrating the various teams involved to realize the business potential in the most empowering ways. Creating executive sponsor support for the important accounts helps strengthen the relationships and the overall network with the customer at multiple levels. We will learn in more detail in chapter 8 how executive sponsors, who we call "growth champions," have an indelible impact on the company's growth through their customer-centric focus.[8]

Schindler, as a key partner for its large contractor customer Larsen & Toubro (L&T) in India, realized that executive sponsor support was a critical factor for its success with the customer. Even though the Triple Fit growth potential in the share of wallet with L&T had been identified as 50 percent from the existing 18 percent, this potential could only be realized if the relationship, which was still transactional, transformed into a strategic one. Schindler needed to convey its value to the customer, not just as one of the many suppliers, but as a strategic one. However, Schindler realized that unsupported relationships could become a momentum killer of growth with not only L&T but several of its strategic customers. To avoid this, it identified the role of the executive sponsor as not only a door opener with the customer to get visibility at the top level but also as a source of strategic alignment through joint KPIs between the two companies. It also mapped a contact matrix for the customer—with department-wise coordinates up to the last level. Thus, creating executive sponsor support was a key factor for Schindler in winning and keeping its most important customers. As a consequence, the pipeline with L&T has substantially improved too.

Momentum killer 3: Communication breakdowns and how to overcome them

The right communication with the customer in an open, fair way not only creates new opportunities but also helps resolve the conflicts associated with the delivery of complex solutions due to a difficult environment or existing operational issues. Using strategic communication as a door opener with the customer through regular customer meetings is a key factor in the successful implementation of a Triple Fit growth plan.

When a supplier we were working with aimed to build a stronger relationship with its customer L'Oréal S.A., a French multinational personal care company focusing on sustainability initiatives, it identified that avoidant communication was a momentum killer of growth with its customer. In the past, the communication was merely focused on requests for proposals (RFPs), leaving little room for a strategic dialogue. Ongoing weekly meetings, which the supplier initiated, became the first communication breakthrough, serving to build credibility with the customer in a new focus area in addition to the existing enzymes business by demonstrating continuous commitment. The creation of an internal customer team was a second key step in achieving this and a requirement for the success of a game-changing communication approach. The supplier continued the communication process in an agile way, seeking customer feedback more deeply in quarterly business reviews. Finally, both companies ran annual Triple Fit reviews that helped them move both businesses forward into new growth areas for co-development of sustainability initiatives, new product development, and mutually beneficial commercial solutions. To overcome the potential momentum killer, supplier companies must proactively engage with their customers at all levels of the relationship, not just send RFP responses.

Back to Miro Milojkovic and his Vodafone team—they overcame each of these momentum killers one by one. At the planning fit level, they already had an ongoing strategic dialogue with Worldcar that had resulted in a strong communication flow between the two companies, eliminating any risk of communication breakdown. But the companies found that their mutual strategies were misaligned and the relationship itself was unsupported without commitment from executive sponsors. Therefore, to align the strategies of the two companies, Milojkovic conceptualized a few pilot projects in the first phase of his growth plan to demonstrate the data-monetization potential of the connected car business in Europe, Africa, and India to Worldcar. In addition, the executive sponsor interventions helped transform the mindsets on both sides from the short- to long-term value-creation perspective and kept the growth momentum alive for mutually beneficial outcomes.

Growth Momentum Killers at the Execution Fit Level

The execution fit level focuses on executing the formulation and delivery of solutions for the customer. A successful Triple Fit growth plan implementation at this level requires: (1) shifting from product-centric thinking to a value cocreation mindset by identifying sources of value beyond the products and defining new value propositions together with the customer; (2) optimizing the supply chain processes to overcome operational inefficiencies and cost overruns, while unlocking new value from more collaborative processes; and (3) creating IT, financial, and legal systems that enable strategic alignment with the customer and resolve obstacles in a timely manner. There are several obstacles to overcome at this level to better respond to the building blocks solutions, processes, and systems. (See figure 6-3.)

FIGURE 6-3

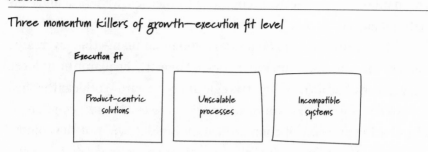

Three momentum killers of growth—execution fit level

Execution fit

| Product-centric solutions | Unscalable processes | Incompatible systems |

Momentum killer 4: Product-centric solutions and how to overcome them

Most company strategies are naturally derived from product portfolios, thus making them product-centric. Enter geographies as a second dimension, and voilà—here is how most companies still do their budget planning and annual reporting. The only dimension that is missing is the customer. As we have shown, putting products before customers is a huge limitation when it comes to finding new sources of growth, which require a shift to a value cocreation mindset with the customers. Shifting from product-centric thinking to a value cocreation mindset happens by identifying sources of value beyond the products and defining new joint value propositions with the customer. This enables solutions that are truly customer-centric.

VAT, an advanced valves provider for the semiconductor industry, takes great pride in its products, which are driven by high-end technology. However, although VAT had a large share of wallet with its customer we will call Atlas, it found that the nature of the relationship was still transactional, requiring heavy focus to protect this share of wallet. Product-centric solutions were the momentum killer of growth for VAT with Atlas. With the changing megatrends in the areas of health care and clean energy, VAT found a strategic fit with Atlas to expand its current product portfolio into life and material sciences. Unlocking these adjacent growth areas would boost its current share of wallet and help maintain it in the long run. However, this needed a complete shift into a value cocreation mindset, as customer inputs were necessary to grow in these new areas and develop innovative solutions. This meant understanding customer pains and jointly developing a multiyear product plan with the customer. Engaging the customer step-by-step in a 360-degree Triple Fit discussion beyond "solutions" was key for overcoming the potential momentum killer. In the long run, VAT will be able to scale up in these new focus areas with other strategic customers as well, creating a sustainable business with above-average profit growth. Thus, shifting out of a product-centric mindset helped VAT identify a significant, untouched business opportunity for organic growth together with its customer.

Momentum killer 5: Unscalable processes and how to overcome them

To deliver the agreed products and services to the customer, a company needs to optimize the processes that enable the delivery. Through challenging times, the strength of the processes is tested, and the companies find out which processes really perform under changing conditions, including growth initiatives. These range from value chain processes to the entire supply chain. The ideal scenario is when the identification of the existing inefficiencies is made clear through customer inputs and feedback, as well as the customer sharing its requirements. Significant cost savings for the customer and for the supplier company are unlocked by eliminating these inefficacies, leading to new growth opportunities. Optimizing the value chain processes to overcome operational inefficiencies and cost overruns, while generating new value from more collaborative processes, is critical to sustaining growth.

Indicia Worldwide, a London-based communications agency, wanted to pivot its historically transactional relationship with their largest global client, Unilever. The companies realized that the performance of in-store retail marketing was largely measured by one single KPI, cost reduction. However, they saw that with investment constantly being reduced, this practice was not sustainable, and the impact of retail marketing would ultimately decline. By implementing a joint business development plan that leveraged the principles of the Triple Fit strategy, their partnership transformed significantly. Through the application of data and technology platforms, marketing materials produced for Unilever could now be tracked, measured, and evaluated in terms of sustainability impact, store placement and sales impact. While year-on-year comparable cost savings achieved for Unilever are still double digit in percentage terms, the measurable upsell effect of optimized "next generation" point-of-sales material surpassed 70 percent on a specific seasonal soup campaign run as a proof-of-concept in China. While for Indicia, the top line revenue with its largest client has remained stable, the bottom-line profitability (as well as the client relationship) has strengthened materially.

Momentum killer 6: Incompatible systems and how to overcome them

Daily business between a supplier and a customer firm runs via various systems, including IT, financial, and legal. If these systems are compatible, business operations run smoothly, and difficult obstacles can be resolved in a timely manner. However, incompatible systems accelerate a communication breakdown and their financial impact is negative. From integrated platforms to aligned KPIs and scorecards to mutual performance tracking to joint risks and rewards—many factors go into bringing systems up-to-date and making them truly effective. Creating IT, financial, and legal systems that enable strategic alignment with the customer further helps resolve obstacles in a timely manner and keeps the growth path clear.

When a German-based chemicals company consulted one of its key clients for a review of its performance, it became clear that despite the long-term strategy to create value for both, the existing systems weren't supporting the realization of the vision. The customer was not receiving clear information on order status or tracking of late deliveries, creating several further challenges, and making incompatible systems a momentum killer of mutual growth. Based on the Triple Fit inputs from the client, the company took corrective measures for the IT systems resolution, put new KPIs into place, and updated the performance measures. This helped identify significant savings for both companies and led to risk mitigation, which in turn helped the supplier to navigate the complex supply chain issues and go all in with its customer.

For Milojkovic and his Vodafone team, the main priorities at the execution level as agreed with Worldcar were to eliminate the product-centric thinking and deliver on the process of pilot projects. One of Milojkovic's key focus areas to overcome the potential roadblocks was to evaluate a single business case per pilot project and compare suitable direct and indirect business models, which involved safety-related services for OEMs. A practical case in point was the conceptualization, with all involved parties, of an airtight process for stolen vehicle recovery after the theft of a car. This helped avoid the potential momentum killers at this stage and secured the relationship.

Growth Momentum Killers at the Resources Fit Level

The resources fit level focuses on making the right resource-allocation decisions by shifting toward a customer-centric organizational design. A successful Triple Fit growth plan implementation at this level requires: (1) creating highly skilled and dedicated customer-facing teams; (2) implementing structures that enable cross-functional alignment to overcome organizational silos and allow all departments to work as one company to serve the customer; and (3) ensuring knowledge sharing for realizing customer-centric innovation opportunities. The obstacles to overcome at this level correspond to the building blocks of people, structures, and knowledge. (See figure 6-4.)

FIGURE 6-4

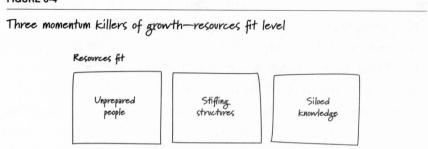

Three momentum killers of growth—resources fit level

Resources fit

Unprepared people	Stifling structures	Siloed knowledge

Momentum killer 7: Unprepared people and how to support them

Success with strategic accounts is achieved through dedicated teams that enable high-value interactions that often change the customer's perception of the company and add value to both organizations. These teams think locally and act globally, enabling collaboration and mutual growth with the strategic accounts. We will learn in more detail in chapter 7 about how sales executives who are customer general managers shape the company's growth through their unfaltering dedication, multilevel capabilities, and the right skills. For now, we conclude that starting a Triple Fit initiative without preparing the people involved can quickly turn into a sobering disappointment.

Consider, for example, the case of a major bank that was preparing to become more customer-centric for its corporate clients. During an in-person workshop with about fifty corporate client managers, the participants were supposed to share their best value-creation stories. After a brief introduction, the first presenter on stage concluded with a proud smile on his face: "I have created value by extending the credit line of my customer from €900 million to €1 billion." The audience applauded, the bank's leaders nodded appreciatively, and our external adviser team was left stunned. About a half-dozen other examples with more or less similar results followed. When we intervened, the client did not receive our polite but straightforward comment about the below-par value-creation approach too well. And not surprisingly, the bank struggled to deliver profitable growth in the following years, because unprepared people in the client-facing teams were a momentum killer of growth. The situation only changed when the leadership team launched two initiatives: First, it made a series of benchmarking visits to successful companies in other industries. Second, a high-caliber coaching program prepared the bank's senior leaders for the future of value creation beyond the classic banking business offers to business customers. Both initiatives became the starting point for a strategic dialogue between better prepared client managers and their corporate clients.

Momentum killer 8: Stifling structures and how to fix them

The right organizational structures enable companies to get things done by ensuring that there is constant cross-functional support across teams and the customer-facing teams can deliver what they have promised to customers. But organizational silos hinder the supplier from working as one company for its customer.[9] The cost efficiencies and growth agendas are not fully realized until all departments are on board to fully support and serve the customer. The goal here is to bridge the silos and create structures that support growth.

When we worked together with a supplier we call StarTrak, who was serving a global retail chain we call Mercatura, we saw that there was significant growth potential waiting to be unlocked. Both companies realized that there was limited interaction between their respective departments and no joint governance teams, thus making stifling structures a potential momentum killer of growth in the relationship. To identify joint business opportunities, StarTrak incorporated more forward-looking discussions with the Mercatura, which were driven through the top management and executive sponsor support and made fruitful with the involvement of the different departments. To align on long-term IT and product requirements with the customer, StarTrak mapped out the stakeholders at different levels and proposed a three-year Triple Fit growth plan driving cross-functional work. Despite a well-established key account organizational struc-ture, StarTrak realized that cost efficiencies and growth potential areas could only be identified by involving the teams with respective expertise in different domains. Over time, the various departments agreed to work together as "One StarTrak" with their respective Mer-catura counterparts and bridged the silos to fully realize the vision of a high-value strategic partnership with the client.

Momentum killer 9: Knowledge silos and how to overcome them

Our research shows that once the focus areas for growth have been identified, continuous knowledge sharing is critical to the realiza-tion of joint innovation plans. Being customer-centric requires an open and transparent relationship between the two firms, and shar-ing knowledge is a key aspect of the equation. Technology by its very nature makes knowledge sharing a necessary part of the customer-centric innovation journey, and this applies to almost all industries and markets.

When Japanese firm Konica Minolta, a leading imaging products and IT services provider, was focusing on delivering innovative solu-tions to one of its customers in the energy sector, it identified siloed knowledge as a potential growth momentum killer. A Triple Fit ex-ercise had led Konica to discover new opportunities in jointly devel-oping state-of-the-art internet of things and AI technologies with the customer. Konica intended to link its efforts to its customer's four strategic key objectives: cost effectiveness, operational stability, fu-ture flexibility, and business strategies. Through the sharing of inno-vation insights, Konica was able to support the customer's vision of a sustainable world through innovation projects that focused on digi-talization opportunities. Thus, knowledge sharing between the two companies helped identify significant cost savings for the customer, creating a win-win solution for both.

For Milojkovic and his Vodafone team, the focus at the resources level was on ensuring that the teams were well prepared and had the right skills to ensure the successful delivery of the project. In order to avoid stifling structures based on traditional hierarchies as a momentum killer, both companies agreed to set up an agile working structure with a flat organization to make quick decisions. Also, they agreed to regularly exchange knowledge through joint forums with the relevant departments and working groups and created a joint database for project collaboration and easy access of information. This enabled Vodafone to create the right allocation of resources for its value-creation initiatives with Worldcar and enabled positive forward momentum for realizing business growth.

Best Practices to Keep the Growth Momentum Going

Based on our fieldwork, we have found the following practices most helpful to keep the growth momentum on track:

- Value-creation projects

- Ninety-day Triple Fit cycles

- Regular Triple Fit pit stops

Let's have a look at each practice in more detail.

Value-creation projects to create reference cases

When embarking for the first time on a Triple Fit initiative, we usually recommend a limited set of five to ten pilot cases to start with. Of course, this is not our own invention, and much has already been written about the value and logic of pilot projects in various contexts.[10] But what's perhaps new is that we have seen these value-creation project pilots succeed more when they were delivered as executive memos written as a business case or what we call a value-creation project consisting of five to ten pages, all written in prose, rather than as a PowerPoint presentation. Prose forces you to think through your

ideas and make logical arguments in a way that bullet points don't—
if anything, presentation style might become a way to mask the fact
you don't have a solid argument. We've reviewed hundreds of these
memos, and while the writing means they are more work, their success rate versus presentations has convinced us they're well worth the
time and effort. They match the way senior executives want to learn
about new customer opportunities. Thus, we pay great attention to
the writing of these business cases.

Maersk, for example, has been using value-creation projects for the
last five years for all its top global customers in a nine-month process
that involves significant management attention and coaching. The
case of Kotahi described in chapter 1 is an example of this initiative.
The following structure of a sample executive memo written as a business case may give you a hint of how you can implement this practice
in your own context and organization:

- Management summary: The game-changer idea and how to
  make it work for which impact

- Triple Fit growth plan: The three sections of analysis, strategy,
  and actions that are customer-validated, as shown in chapter 5

  - Analysis: Triple Fit ratings, financial facts and figures,
    further data from account plan

  - Strategy: The jointly developed Triple Fit story with
    central message, key asks, and consequences of approval
    (or nonapproval)

  - Actions: Making the game-changer work on a timeline, con-
    siderations to mitigate implementation risks, contingency
    planning

- Identification of a business case for growth: The detailed
  outline of the plan leading to a solid business case backed by
  financials and including both growth opportunities and the
  risks of not moving forward with the project

- The project pitch: Engaging one's organization and the customer's organization in sequential steps and getting executive sponsor commitment on the project, resulting in a value-creation project pitch, which is presented to key stakeholders

- Appendix: Backup information, detailed financial calculations, simulation data, or similar document(s), that will support the case

Our data shows that completed value-creation projects and executive memos create a minimum payback ranging from $1 million to $100 million within less than twelve months. We have seen in all the companies we worked with almost *no* alternatives that delivered the same payback. So, the value-creation projects become a handy tool to kick-start the transition to value creation.

Ninety-day Triple Fit cycles to harvest quick wins

Once the value-creation projects are in motion, they are usually flanked by Triple Fit workshops or interviews (described in chapter 5). Now comes a crucial phase in the Triple Fit process. Based on more than ten thousand cases we have supported so far, we conclude that the most successful companies deliberately invested time and manpower to keep the activities on track. Without this, there is a high risk that the initially launched efforts may run out of steam quickly. Consider, for example, the case of a global insurance company we call Risk Protection Experts (RPE). After discovering the Triple Fit canvas as a meaningful tool to take its corporate relationships to the next level, RPE embarked on a set of ten Triple Fit pilot cases. Due to resource constraints, however, RPE did not commit to the effort of value-creation projects, which left the ten client managers charged with the Triple Fit activities somewhat in despair. As an alternative, we recommended running regular reviews and coaching. Unfortunately, this effort was also declined, and the whole Triple Fit initiative, which first showed some promising results, stalled.

In our research, the ideal window for revisiting account plans based on the Triple Fit process is ninety days. The reason is simple: the ninety-day quick-win actions formulated in step four of the Triple Fit process are up for review after a quarter and need revisiting with new inputs. Ninety days is the right length of time to ensure that the plan stays flexible and can address all contingencies that may arise as well as revisit the market opportunities that present themselves. In a ninety-day period, the Triple Fit process sequence can be broken down into three four-week sprints, like the logic of agile workflows.[11] We have observed that it usually takes about four weeks to complete the five Triple Fit steps, with customer-validated input starting a questionnaire and meetings for developing the input to the steps. Ninety days is also adequate time for execution, which begins from the moment the stakeholders have approved and committed to the next actions. The ninety-day cycles can also lead to groundbreaking discoveries at the implementation stage of the business strategy.

An interesting case in point is the experience of a pharmaceutical company we were advising on its future go-to-market strategy. When we arrived at the third ninety-day Triple Fit cycle, the sales leader team also invited its then CEO. After ten presentations of validated Triple Fit growth plans of fifteen minutes each, he stood up and looked around, stating, "We have now heard ten times that the customer is asking for a completely different approach than we are currently offering in our strategy. Guess who must change?" Fortunately, all relevant stakeholders not only were in the room but also committed to take the voice of the customer into account, and the company enjoyed an above-industry growth for the next decade. From a business strategy logic, the pharma company also learned that its ninety-day Triple Fit reviews helped to create an early warning system that created game-changer insights. In essence, the ninety-day Triple Fit reviews presented joint value-creation strategies with leading indicators predicting new problems rather than analyzing lagging indicators that revealed old ones.

Triple Fit pit stops to foster peer learning

Triple Fit ratings should usually be updated once every twelve months. It's fine if customers request earlier updates, but we recommend not doing it more often than every six months. Realistically speaking, what is the point of ninety-day quick wins when there is a constant rating process going on? It's better to agree on a slower pace for the ratings but keep an eye on the implementation of mutually beneficial actions and projects. Thus, the final tool we spotlight is regular pit stops between the ninety-day Triple Fit reviews.

Conducting a Triple Fit pit stop is simple but can work wonders, sometimes with the help of an external coach, even when the coached participant has no trust in the process or doubts that the exercise will deliver value beyond obvious chatter. We experienced this push-back, for example, when our team was coaching an account manager who was calling on Mars Petfood as a customer. When he started his monthly pit-stop coaching, the Triple Fit ratings from Mars were more favorable than those from the supplier, despite very transactional behavior on the customer's side. Of course, the coaching discussion centered around how to explain such ratings—were they simply courtesy ratings or did the customer perhaps overlook something? In a first reaction, the proposal of the account manager was to not address this discrepancy to avoid waking up sleeping dogs. No sales rep wants to openly admit to weakness.

But thanks to many reference cases in our library, our coaching team could point out that exactly the opposite approach would deliver the highest value. So they advised the account manager to explain to his customer the full truth in the Triple Fit picture, even though this meant challenging some of the favorable customer assumptions. To the surprise of the account manager, the customer thanked him for not selling weaknesses as strengths and committed to a joint task force, addressing the shortcomings in the most critical momentum-killer areas for mutual benefit. After six months, the relationship started to turn from transactional to partnership style, and both companies embarked on a much closer collaboration with significant business results only one year after the monthly coaching. In later chapters, we will explain how to embody these best practices in your daily business life to become an integral part of your customers' strategies.

TAKEAWAYS

- Nine momentum killers can block the growth momentum; overcoming all of them is crucial for future success of your Triple Fit initiative.

- Value-creation projects, summarized in form of a short executive memo, are a pragmatic approach to demonstrate the proof of concept of your Triple Fit initiative.

- Ninety-day Triple Fit cycles combined with targeted coaching during Triple Fit pit stops help realize quick wins and drive mutual success further.

REFLECTION QUESTIONS

- Which of the nine momentum killers do you see across your customer relationships?

- Which of the best practices would add value to your organization and keep your growth momentum on track?

- What could be the themes of one to two pilot value-creation projects for your company? Go to triplefitstrategy.com for illustrative examples of value creation project themes.

SUSTAINING TRIPLE FIT CONDITIONS

CHAPTER 7

DEVELOP CUSTOMER GENERAL MANAGERS

In part I, we looked at understanding Triple Fit trajectories and how to start the strategic dialogue. In part II, we focused on navigating Triple Fit journeys and how to execute validated growth plans. Now, in part III, we will turn our attention to sustaining Triple Fit conditions. In particular, we will be looking at the protagonists that have to master the transition from product selling to value creation at both the customer and the organizational levels. Two roles are essential for making Triple Fit strategy work in business relationships: first, the many salespeople orchestrating value creation at the front line (chapter 7), and second, their managers providing the favorable conditions for sustained success (chapter 8).

Some years ago, Catherine,* a client manager working for a large logistics company we'll call International Cargo Group (ICG), was charged with what many in her supplier firm considered a mission impossible: grow ICG's business with a leading aircraft manufacturer we will call Volantis beyond its current, very low share of wallet. At the time, projects between Volantis and various ICG business units were

* Name disguised.

taking place primarily at the local level and with varying intensity, so Catherine decided to take a dual approach. First, she would honor the relationship that had existed between ICG and Volantis for more than twenty-five years and visit customer contacts personally, something her predecessors hadn't done. Second, she would address the business potential by focusing on the deals she could really win, not just any request for proposal that came along.

ICG had a dedicated program to serve important customers, but Catherine's plan went beyond the program's guidelines and aimed for a real strategic dialogue between the two companies. From an in-depth analysis of the customer's business drivers in the relationship, Catherine initiated connections between top-ranked executives from both companies. Building relationships at multiple levels helped make the customer opportunity visible across ICG. She also developed and validated a pilot program with her customer for a new service approach in the aerospace industry. To achieve buy-in internally, Catherine coached ICG business units for better internal collaboration. Twice per year, for example, she organized a global road show for all involved units, where she presented the latest updates and got the local units to set their support capacity for Volantis. She also ensured that customer representatives could meet their ICG counterparts at the local and regional levels, which sometimes required creative use of internal budgets for this very purpose. In some cases, the HQ marketing department travel budget for trade shows was used for sending the extended sales teams instead.

Of course, there were challenges—in particular, the need to sharpen reporting and communication on a global scale and to overcome silo thinking and turf battles. But both organizations benefited from an open and honest approach from the start, allowing them to build trust continuously. Catherine knew she had uncovered customer upside when one Volantis rep said to her, "In case you can solve our issues here, you can have the rest of the [business] volume, too." However, her work did not stop there. Catherine made no secret of the fact that the team would like to become the leading logistics partner for the full range of aerospace and defense businesses in the Volantis Group, with a global presence and the capability to service and manage the most complex operations.

To achieve this goal, Catherine convinced her senior leaders to accept shared risk models and implement a global team for this business relationship, consisting of a dozen members working full-time on this major account. As her marshaling of resources and orchestrating of both value-creation and risk management efforts continued, the results confirmed the impact of her approach: she achieved twenty times revenue growth in less than five years, while also creating a replicable logistics solution for the aerospace industry she could take to other B2B partners.

Of course, the notion that customers are important assets of a company and therefore need special attention isn't novel, but it's crucial to manage those assets well in a world where many customers are reducing their number of B2B partners over the last decades. Volantis, for example, reduced its supplier portfolio by 80 percent from three thousand to five hundred.[1] Walmart now accounts for 15 percent of P&Gs total sales, more than $12 billion.[2] One wonders whether companies are really prepared to handle such heavyweight business via the old-style product-selling approach. Previous research has addressed supplier-customer relationships primarily from a sales technique and negotiation perspective. But so far, no one has explicitly studied supplier-customer *value creation* and *risk reduction* as core activities at the individual business relationship level. The pivotal question yet to be answered is: How can salespeople systematically create value and reduce risk *with customers*, and what are the related managerial implications of doing that?

The Two Roles of Customer Management

We set out to investigate what such a concentration of customers meant not only for the approach to manage them in the daily business, but also how to manage—or better mitigate—the risk exposure resulting from these customers.[3] In a research project conducted by Christoph in collaboration with Axel Thoma from University of St. Gallen and George Yip, then at CEIBS Shanghai, we identified eighteen industries that showed strong signs of customer consolidation, including advertising, banking, consumer goods, chemicals, defense, IT, logistics, pharmaceuticals, and industrial machinery.[4] All companies in the sample granted the research team full access to their sales force and financial figures. Based on multiple qualification rounds, we ended up with more than one hundred best-in-class cases. We contrasted these cases with the ten thousand cases in our research database and found that the extreme roles—the low and the high performers—had significantly different characteristics. We call the low performers "vendors" and the high performers "orchestrators."

Let's look at each.

The vendor role

Salespeople who apply a product-market fit perspective consider the customer a sales generator and often act as simple order-takers. They typically attempt to sell more of the same items while protecting their prices and margins. Their approach is unilateral, shorter term, and arm's length, as well as strictly professional. The customer manager's main activities include analyzing the customer buying organization, exploring and meeting customer needs, and enhancing stakeholder relationships. These activities aim to build credibility and trust over time (primarily through procurement), obtain a greater share of the customer's business wallet, and ensure partnership continuity through higher switching costs.

Vendor salespeople tend to regard themselves as the sales owner— the "Lone Ranger" who closes deals. To achieve their sales targets, they participate in product selling: matching customer needs with their firm's existing products and services.

Our research cites the product-market fit perspective as a suitable go-to-market approach for transactional supplier-customer relationships, which do not have to be adversarial, but which lack the drive to cocreate new value. Overall, the product-market perspective offers only a limited turnaround through value-creation efforts because its value and risk focus are limited, supplier-centric, and short-term-oriented.

In addition, customer managers who adopt a vendor perspective might not always be able to put the business relationship first. Short-term sales targets are enhanced by a deep analysis of the customer's lifetime value for the supplier. To position the supplier as a value-adding partner, customer managers often attempt to become a kind of adviser, applying consultative techniques to determine the customer's pain points and then using these insights to develop tailored value propositions. Metrics such as customer satisfaction and loyalty (and, of course, bottom-line results) determine relationship success and partnership status. However, this advisory role still falls short of the value creation orchestrators achieve because it's still product centered.

The orchestrator role

Customer managers who define, explore, and create value within the wider supplier-customer ecosystem adopt the orchestrator perspective. They define, pursue, and exchange more comprehensively than in the product-market perspective. Through collaboration and matched firm-specific resources and competencies, two firms create value that no one entity can achieve alone; they share and control for risks, too. Orchestrators maintain a continuous stream of insights about the market, the competition, the customer's business, and how the supplier's products, services, and capabilities can change the economics of the customer's business model. They possess strong conceptual and financial abilities that enable them to recognize customer business drivers and translate them into joint value-creation projects. They also advocate business cases to multiple levels of *both* organizations, build commitment that leads to action, and marshal required resources across the network. An important indicator of value creation is whether a supplier helps its customer become more competitive and successful in its market. Orchestrator salespeople are often characterized as "intrapreneurs."[5]

An example of a well-applied orchestrator role is the case of a supplier we call ColoraTech (CT) with regard to one of its customers, a multinational company in the paint and performance coatings industry. In the past, different CT units laterally delivered to the customer, fulfilling customers' needs on the basis of their product portfolio and unit strategy. Because of the size of the business, each unit installed a key account manager, who coordinated the business relationship along with other key accounts and attempted to grow the business from a single-unit, product-market perspective. To get beyond this, CT's top management introduced group-level account managers who were responsible for the most important customers. These group account managers orchestrated different activities and actors at a higher level and explored the business relationship and its risks. They neither replaced nor commanded the unit-based key account managers. Instead, they provided an additional resource to them.

In CT's relationship with the customer, the group account manager helped save a business relationship at risk and also drove a new value cocreation project. The customer faced an internal initiative to consolidate the production of certain coatings from multiple locations into a single site. The consolidation raised operational concerns because the chosen site was in a residential area with limited room for expansion. Considering these space limitations and the project complexity, the customer wondered how it could cope. The company even considered relocating its production out of Europe, which would have had serious negative implications for CT's current business.

Without an orchestrator perspective, CT might not have become aware of this development. But since that person did hear about the challenge, the orchestrator was able to convene a group with reps from both companies to make the process more efficient. The outcome was a cocreated, integrated mixing system. Through this cocreated solution, the customer's laboratory spending was reduced 30 percent, and it managed space more efficiently and increased flexibility to produce smaller batches more quickly. CT in turn benefited from additional cross-unit sales of additives, effect pigments, and measurement instruments; it also gained a reputation as a value contributor and strategic partner for the customer, beyond a single served site.

. . .

When comparing both roles, there are several differences to note (see figure 7-1). A vendor salesperson's mindset is to focus on the current share of wallet with the customer. To increase the share of wallet or in broader terms—the share of the accessible business—this salesperson focuses on market growth and pursues activities to help shift business from other competitors, such as compelling pricing or more appealing products and services. The growth potential here is limited, and it feels a bit like making the "red ocean mistake" at the level of a single business relationship.[6] Entering price wars is never a good idea.[7]

In contrast, the orchestrator role extends beyond short-term sales tactics. A true orchestrator's mindset focuses on value creation for both the customer and the supplier firms, for example, by taking care

FIGURE 7-1

Two roles of customer management

The vendor	The orchestrator
Focus on growing the share of wallet of existing business	Focus on growing wallet beyond existing business
Quarterly reviews with procurement	Joint strategic dialogue across the industry ecosystem
Internally developed and agreed-upon 12-month forecasts	Jointly developed, customer validated 3-year growth road maps
Handover to operations/fulfillment	Marshaling resources to ensure proper execution
Preferred pricing and extended contract terms	Shared governance with regular top-manager interaction

of areas that are not necessarily in the scope of the classic salesperson's job description, such as marshaling resources for seamless execution. Think of Catherine at ICG calling on Volantis. She was only successful by acting as an orchestrator between both companies and covering all nine aspects of the Triple Fit canvas.

We are often asked which role should be applied when. Aren't there also scenarios when an orchestrator role would be overkill? And what do you do when the customer is only interested in negotiation, not collaboration? The short answer is that on some occasions the vendor role may be sufficient. However, increasingly, technology, not people, can play this role. The trend in B2B sales is pointing toward fewer but more upskilled sales roles, as automated or even autonomous sales processes increasingly take over low-level transactions that were historically covered by the human order-takers we label vendors.[8]

Based on the analysis of the ten thousand cases in our database, firms should consider the following as indicators that it's time to change role behavior from vendor to orchestrator:

- A strategic customer tells you that you could make x-times more business with it if you got your act together.

- One or more of your local market or business units frequently kills business that would be beneficial to the entire company.

- You are convinced that you are producing and delivering superior value, but your top customers do not see it the same way.

- There is tangible value-creation potential for the customer, but your conversations are primarily with procurement about prices and volumes.

- You have no one dedicated to bringing the customer strategy into your own organization.

Any given customer manager likely cannot shift easily between vendor and orchestrator mindsets because they demand considerably different skill sets and mandates. Our findings suggest that most B2B salespeople aren't orchestrators. In our sample, only 20 percent of salespeople were in the orchestrator mode. This spread is a matter of concern because today's customers deliberately work with fewer suppliers and expect those that remain to offer closer cocreation-based business relationships, with dedicated counterparts in the supplier firm.

Four Advantages of Orchestrators

Having managers at the customer interface who adopt an orchestrator perspective for strategic customers in collaborative business relationships increases four types of advantages for the supplier:

- Relationship advantage

- Commercial advantage

- Knowledge advantage

- Leadership advantage

Our review of all business cases that sought to create value for both the supplier and the customer revealed that those orchestrators with the highest performance outcomes covered all four areas in an integrated way.

Relationship advantage. The relationship challenge arises with customers that account for significant amounts of a supplier's total business, often more than 30 percent. This core business must be protected, because losing and regaining customers is much more costly than retaining them. Global buyers are facing geographically and functionally complex decision-making and influence networks. Building multilevel relationships and trust takes years, whereas harming them requires just seconds. The differentiating factor here is the orchestrator perspective for building broader and deeper relationships: The customer manager must have regular access to executive suite managers and a multilevel network as a recognized partner for strategic dialogue or sparring and joint value creation.

Rather than being just a golf buddy, the customer manager must be able to identify key stakeholders and their individual motivations so that they can nurture these relationships. A case in point of a well-executed relationship advantage with an orchestrator mindset is the story of Patrice Spinner, a longtime global account director at Marriott Hotels. As a result of the 9/11 attack on New York's Twin Towers, Deloitte & Touche (D&T) lost, in one tragic day, its central office in the United States. Hundreds of employees had no access to their offices in the busiest season of the year.[9] Marriott itself was affected by travel bans. When D&T sent out a request for proposal for a temporary office space, Spinner went for the game-changer orchestrator approach. Within forty-eight hours, she drummed up all relevant stakeholders and submitted a solution beyond the RFP requirements. The offer included a full-service contract for rooms, safety and security systems, food and beverage, telecommunication, and office equipment at the (empty) Marriott Marquis Hotel in Times Square. Spinner even had the Marriott staff trained to answer the phone calls in D&T's name. The value created for both organizations was evident, and customer loyalty reached a new height for many years after Spinner's game-changer relationship move.

Commercial advantage. The commercial challenge arises because supplier-customer partnerships incur costs to develop their relationship, govern it, and then pursue and implement joint projects. The differentiating factor for an orchestrator is their ability to do more than just sell more of the same or gain more share of the customer's wallet. Managers who adopt an orchestrator perspective consider the supplier-customer relationship from a deeper commercial perspective, exploring total partnership costs and devising measures to lower these costs, then applying concepts such as total cost of ownership to address hidden costs and value drivers.

For its most strategic customers, a global IT company appointed orchestrator client directors who were responsible for a global customer as a business with its own profit-and-loss and dedicated organization.

In turn, these client directors had the motivation to create new business fields, run the business relationship efficiently, and eliminate system costs. Customer managers at a household appliances firm similarly were trained to understand both their financial system and that of the customer so that they could identify, connect, and leverage joint value and cost drivers.

Knowledge advantage. The knowledge challenge occurs because suppliers must go well beyond superior product quality and performance. Customers no longer buy products or services; they seek knowledge-based value that makes them more competitive. Merely probing and catering to customer needs is not sufficient in cocreation business relationships, nor are customer relationship management systems that rely on automated knowledge creation and application. Managers that adopt an orchestrator perspective are not only expert listeners and information gatherers, but also knowledge orchestrators who translate information that is critical to value creation and risk management, from inside out and outside in. With their intricate knowledge of value system drivers and the competences of both the customer and their own organization, such managers can identify, specify, and initiate new value projects, together with customers.

A case in point comes from a major supplier of store shelving and fittings that was able to help a leading UK supermarket chain. With in-depth knowledge of customer strategy, the global account manager initiated an innovation partnership, including an innovation council and dedicated R&D teams, to develop a new shelf system in six months, a project that normally takes one to two years. The customer obtained a tailored shelf system faster with limited exclusivity; the supplier was able to share its R&D investments, ensure commercialization, and multiply its product range by using the project as the basis for a new product family.

Leadership advantage. The leadership challenge stems from the need for leadership at both team and organizational levels to manage customers. More and more companies declare that the customer-centric or even customer-driven enterprise is their business credo. However, they are unable to walk the talk without leaders who drive and institutionalize this change in their mindset and way of doing business. Orchestrating a global customer relationship for value creation and risk management requires leadership everywhere, not just coordination and administration somewhere in headquarters. Managers that adopt an orchestrator perspective form, motivate, and coach (often virtually) cross-function, cross-unit, and cross-geography teams. They drive alignment among stakeholders and engage them in a value-adding manner. Because team members are often not direct reports, managers at the customer interface must achieve impact without formal authority, based instead on their knowledge, relationship network, and integrity.

For example, a global account manager at a wind-power solutions provider was working with a multinational energy firm. This customer intended to spend several billion euros to build twenty-gigawatt wind energy capacity across multiple markets. However, the wind-power company was structured by geography, so its financing policies and service agreements obstructed a global collaboration with the energy company. The wind-power global account manager, demonstrating intrapreneurial behavior, developed a collaboration memorandum to validate the

FIGURE 7-2

The four skill areas of orchestrators

1 Relationship advantage

Orchestrating multilevel relationships and strategic dialogue to build trust, marshal critical resources, and obtain timely decisions

2 Commercial advantage

Managing the supplier–customer partnership as a dyad in a larger value ecosystem to work against other, competing entities and their offerings

3 Leadership advantage

Rallying support and developing teams for clients while fostering customer-centric thinking and behavior across the organization

4 Knowledge advantage

Obtaining deep insights into customer strategies and business drivers and translating them into value-creating and risk-reducing measures business case for growth, set up a task force of technicians to resolve issues in places where the local markets could not or did not want to provide the needed service, and coached new global account managers about how to build their internal networks and what measures to take to have a strategic dialogue with their customers. These moves resulted in above-average business despite adversarial industry conditions.

Based on these four skills areas, we have developed a list of characteristics that describe the profile of the orchestrator in more detail. Companies can use this list as a starting point to evaluate the skill gaps and necessary training modules:

- Relationship advantage

    - Multilevel networking including C-level connections

    - Impactful stakeholder communication

    - Arbitration and negotiation prowess

- Commercial advantage

    - Financial proficiency

    - Intrapreneurial proficiency and opportunity focus

    - Joint business planning

- Knowledge advantage

    - Strategic and visionary

    - Creativity and systems thinking

    - Business intelligence application and multiplication

- Leadership advantage

    - Individual leadership brand and track record

    - Team development and leadership

    - Influence without authority

Three Key Dimensions to the Orchestrator Perspective—a Guide to Action

Our research has shown various practices for developing orchestrators that fall into three key dimensions: mindset, context, and competence. When these dimensions are all missing, all four types of advantage (relationship, commercial, knowledge, and leadership) earn low ratings, so it is best to consider all three dimensions for leveraging the orchestrator perspective.

Mindset. Developing and deploying managers with an orchestrator perspective requires creating favorable organizational conditions for encouraging the right mindset. The mindset of a salesperson guides their daily behavior and choices; in turn, this mindset depends on the organizational culture. The culture of the firm must not be just product-oriented but also customer-oriented. Otherwise, it will also be necessary to work at levels beyond single customer relationships to turn the company ship in the right direction. We will elaborate on this in chapter 9. What might sound obvious in theory is often arduous for organizations: not all customers are equal, and those that are of strategic importance from an economic viewpoint should be treated as the firm's most vital assets. In a packaging company we have worked with, for example, the customer's claims-handling process was done on a first-come, first-served basis for every customer, regardless of whether a customer accounted for a couple of thousand or several hundred million dollars in annual revenues. Until the firm instilled a customer-oriented mindset, the employees operated by the credo "all customers are kings," or "acoustic priority setting," which led to precarious situations with some of its strategic customers that were decisive for the future success.

The mindset of the orchestrator also results in differentiated go-to-market approaches for various customer segments, including corresponding actors, activities, and resources deployed from the supplier's side. The emergence of yet another role—that of customer managers adopting an orchestrator perspective—can mistakenly seem like a threat to existing (sales) functions, one that increases complexity and potential centralism in debates about who owns the customer. As the examples in our research demonstrate, neither is a concern if the orchestrators, those in charge of leading them, and those who support activities at the front end have the right mindset. Network-oriented managers do not take a supervisory role or create bottlenecks at the group level; they provide different capabilities to drive value creation and risk management in cocreation business relationships in close collaboration with internal and external stakeholders, often without formal authority to command supplier resources. Nor are orchestrators replacing other customer-facing roles, unless those roles represent a less suitable approach.

For example, until recently a multinational technology firm defined and deployed two major sales functions: sales reps and key account managers. When it adopted a more fine-grained approach to the customer portfolio, this tech firm was able to define in detail which platform, in terms of actors, activities, and resources, to deploy for each customer type in its portfolio. As a result, the sales force functions expanded to include additional roles, such as technical key account managers, corporate account managers, and industry cluster managers.

The good news is that changing mindsets does not necessarily cost a lot of money. The bad news is that it means leaving a comfort zone, which requires persistent effort to sustain cognitive and behavioral change. Companies in our research resorted to different means to get there. One approach was to conduct foundational events to launch customer management efforts and introduce the role of the orchestrator. In a formal transformational event, the supplier can create a sense of urgency, change, and appreciation of the new. Companies that have successfully introduced orchestrators hold regular forums to allow customer managers, together with senior management, to explore value-creation projects with important customers that seek cocreation. These results then are shared across the organization to validate existing ideas and demonstrate the value added by the orchestrator perspective. Other companies introduce top executive relationship management processes to engage senior management in the formulation of customer strategies and initiate validated co-creation projects. For example, in an integrated technology firm we worked with, customer assets that were part of the top executive relationship management program achieved twice as many sales as other accounts, driven by new value projects as a result of the application of the orchestrator perspective.

Context. Many companies must also fix a context problem, such as when the objectives and incentives for personnel development are misaligned or if they have tried to resolve a personnel problem with organizational redesign. Distinguishing whether the problem relates to the context or to people is essential for determining the right remedy. Our research suggests that orchestrators deployed in an organization with a visible and supportive platform (e.g., customer management program) can harness the right organizational support and resources relevant to their context.

Among the companies that installed orchestrators, three measures stand out as particularly successful for setting context.

One, they set a clear mandate with specific responsibilities, measures, and collaboration norms for orchestrators. Collaboration does not happen naturally, so explicating connected roles and demonstrating the benefits of the network approach to those who contribute is important. Some firms not only developed a formal written mandate, but also ensured that their top managers communicated and advocated it. For example, a firm that appointed an orchestrator sent a formal letter of inauguration to all division and business unit heads, introducing the person and reinforcing the manager's role as an orchestrator at the front end who could count on the full support of top management.

Two, they set rules of engagement for managing customers as assets in order to avoid turf battles and streamline the process of bringing new team members on board. These guides combined process protocols, clarifications of important questions (e.g., "Who owns the customer?" or "Who has the right to set prices for a strategic customer?"), and explanations of conciliation and escalation procedures in the case of conflicts at the front end.

Three, they align targets and rewards. For many companies, compensation schemes are a "do not touch" area that creates a massive obstacle for institutionalizing managers with an orchestrator perspective. Intrinsic motivation and ad hoc rewards may work in the short term, but orchestrator compensation must reflect the role and its objectives. Instituting a sales incentive plan would mean hoping for A (e.g., the pursuit of longer-term, new value projects that other supplier units help implement) while incentivizing B (e.g., short-term sales deals closed by a specific customer manager). Traditional sales and relationship metrics (such as volume, prices, customer satisfaction, and loyalty scores) are not the best indicators of an orchestrator's performance. Some of the firms we observed tracked performance based on differential value created for the customer, the quantification of new value projects, risks associated with the strategic account in a joint business plan, or the achievement of objectives in a joint supplier-customer scorecard validated by the customer.

Competence. Without skilled orchestrators in place at the right time, a firm can achieve little traction. The question that arises is not only whether to make or buy orchestrators, but also how to define the mission-critical competencies of a high-impact orchestrator, and then determine how to develop and refine them. Orchestrators must possess (or acquire) relationship skills that extend beyond networking with their customer counterparts. Orchestrators who drive cocreation span multilevel networks, up to top management levels, through their deep understanding of what matters to these diverse stakeholders, and then adapt their style of communication accordingly. Good orchestrators can enter strategic dialogues, win share of mind, and arbitrate win-win-win outcomes to marshal critical resources and obtain timely cocreation decisions.

Furthermore, orchestrators must possess a deep commercial understanding of the value drivers of all entities in a relationship. For a sales rep, it may suffice to understand market and customer growth rates, production capacities, and the pricing mechanisms of products and services, and then develop related sales forecasts and supplier-driven action plans. Comprehending the larger value system also requires financial proficiency to draw value maps based on analyses of a customer's business model. These insights then translate into business cases that quantify the differential value created for the supplier and customer, including investment considerations and risk scenarios. Some firms we observed cited such intrapreneurial behavior, describing the manager's ability to act as an entrepreneur who takes ownership of developing the business through opportunity orientation, tolerance for uncertainty, and adaptability.

Orchestrators are competent knowledge brokers as well. To engage high-level stakeholders in a strategic dialogue, they must be able to process relevant business intelligence and prepare it in a compelling manner. In many instances, this knowledge is not readily available from marketing departments or even the customer, because the orchestrator works across functional, geographical, and enterprise boundaries and dives into new areas that promise cocreation opportunities. Being strategic, visionary, and able to think creatively and across systems helps customer managers obtain deep insights into customer strategies and business drivers and translate them into value-creation and risk-reduction activities.

Finally, an orchestrator needs leadership skills that represent perhaps the largest distinction from other sales functions. Most salespeople work independently, according to personal sales quotas; they may collaborate closely with sales support, but they rarely are in a situation in which they lead virtual, multidisciplinary teams. In contrast, orchestrators enable value creation and risk management with customers across multiple teams and units. Their impact depends on their ability to build, lead, coach, and develop an effective, multidisciplinary team that might include customer staff as well. On the one hand, they need the ability to motivate and influence people in the absence of formal authority. On the other hand, successful customer managers understand the importance of developing their individual leadership brand to strengthen their posture in a particular supplier-customer business relationship and for the customer management approach overall. An individual leadership brand might, for example, consist of intellectual capital, social networks, personality, mission, and style.

Customer General Managers: Anchoring the Orchestrator Perspective

Considering the skills required of an orchestrator, we need to find ways to develop them. The observations from our research suggest that talent management efforts for orchestrators are often underestimated. Common challenges include the inability to hire externally due to the absence of qualified candidates and the need for customer managers to have existing relationship networks within the firm; the unsuccessful promotion of great salespeople to orchestrator roles, because of their different skills and personal work preferences; and expectations among high performers that they will move up the career ladder, whereas in reality it takes time to become a true orchestrator.

Companies therefore need to recognize that, as with any new role, there is no predetermined path to develop this new breed of customer managers. Several approaches have worked for the companies we observed. For example, some firms required that anyone who aimed to take a senior management role needed to have several years of experience in customer management, with direct involvement in value cocreation together with a firm's strategic customers. Others preferred a mix of formal training, coaching, and on-the-job applications, acknowledging the complexity of the skills that customer managers need to develop and reinforce over time.

Such skill development programs require subject expertise at the front end (i.e., the customer management program), combined with development tools from human resources management. In many cases, existing leadership and finance programs within organizations should be open to orchestrators, too. Moreover, some firms have used teams of veteran customer managers and senior managers to coach network managers; in one case, a program set up with strategic customers allowed senior management from both the supplier and customer organizations to coach customer managers and supply chain managers. Finally, one company enjoyed great success in developing a successor for an existing customer manager by planning a lengthy transition period that helped ensure the successor could absorb the multilevel network relationships and tacit knowledge.

Using Triple Fit Strategy to Be an Orchestrator

In today's dynamic business-to-business environment, marked by buyer consolidation and price pressures, suppliers must consider their customers as important firm assets to be proactively managed, thus creating value and reducing associated risks. For those strategic supplier-customer relationships in which both parties seek cocreation, the orchestrator perspective—with its deeper levels of value creation and risk management—offers higher growth potential and competitive advantages that neither party could achieve on its own. However, the orchestrator perspective requires a new breed of managers at the front end. These managers should have the mandate, mindset, and skill to act as seasoned conductors who lead interdisciplinary teams and orchestrate resources internally and externally, such that joint value is created and risk gets reduced efficiently and effectively, resulting in new value projects that justify the investment in the orchestrator perspective.

In essence, and as some of the firms we researched stated, the role of an orchestrator is that of a customer general manager. This title might at first appear bold; however, it reflects the mandate and skill set required, very similar to those demanded of a general manager in terms of the relational, commercial, knowledge management, and leadership skills involved. A customer general manager does not take ownership of the customer but rather takes full responsibility for orchestrating and enabling value creation and risk management with the customer along the lines of the 360-degree Triple Fit perspective. Such orchestrations must be achieved without the formal power to command activities at the customer interface. Thus, the general management title subsumes various role elements, such as cross-functional working, multilevel leadership, value and risk considerations as core activity drivers, long-term planning horizons, opportunity ownership, adaptability, and ability to cope with uncertainty. Triple Fit is a valuable guiding map for any customer general manager in identifying and enabling value-creation potential with their strategic customers and orchestrating the unfolding of sustainable growth.

Nicolas Seegmuller is just such a customer general manager, an orchestrator at the highest level. When his Austrian-based food company Agrana, majority-owned by Südzucker Group and Raiffaisen Bank, wanted to transform its relationship with its largest customer, Danone, he used Triple Fit to figure out how and then used all his orchestration skills to make it happen. Using the Triple Fit canvas, he saw that the key priorities would be in planning fit, with a focus on strategies, relationships, and communication. Using his orchestration skills, he took three actions. First, he launched a stream of strategic projects. Second, he mapped all the entities and functions that would be involved in the projects. Third, he engaged the right stakeholders at the right time, in the right way.

It was not easy—the orchestrator role never is—but after eighteen months, Seegmuller got the top leaders from his company and his customer's company together for a meeting, which led to a strategic dialogue. They granted privileged access to each other's business briefings. They cofinanced projects to develop markets together. And Seegmuller got his CEO to be the executive sponsor for the relationship. It was masterful orchestration all around.

But a caveat—companies should not become complacent. A case in point is the example of P&G and Walmart. Described in many textbooks and even a Harvard Business School case as one of *the most* collaborative relationships of the past few decades, this relationship had its ups and downs.[10] In particular, one lesson shows the importance of an ongoing presence of the orchestrator as we proposed it in this chapter. Let's recapitulate the P&G–Walmart story:

When Tom Muccio, then president of global customer teams for Procter & Gamble, was charged in 1986 with transforming the relationship of P&G with Walmart, he knew that this would not be an easy feat. Historically, P&G's relationship with Walmart was transactional and, in some cases, even adversarial and driven by its internal processes. But the numbers were looking good, and revenue was already in the range of $350 million per year. So, from a high-level perspective, all seemed to be on track.

But Muccio knew that P&G was tough to do business with, especially for customers like Walmart. Furthermore, although sales were growing because of Walmart's growth, P&G's market share was low in comparison to the national US market share. The P&G team also had little knowledge of what was going on within Walmart and the retail environment in general. An eye-opening moment came when Muccio compared the Walmart relationship to large P&G markets like Japan. Both businesses were about the same size. But while P&G covered Japan with more than 200 employees, Walmart had only thirteen employees assigned to it across the whole P&G group. This insight was quite shocking and sparked much internal discussion, as it reflected P&G's strong product and brand focus and a lack of the same type of customer focus. To further grow the business with Walmart, Muccio concluded that a significant investment in a new coverage model was necessary.

In his first pitch to then CEO John Pepper, Muccio, playing the role of orchestrator, asked for a team of more than twenty-five full-time people with different backgrounds at the customer headquarters. At first, P&G's management was concerned that these employees would become Walmart employees. But this did not happen at all, and John Pepper eventually became Muccio's number one growth champion (we will describe the role of the growth champion in more detail in chapter 8). Muccio also involved product managers more closely in the dialogue with the customer and agreed on additional, fully dedicated Walmart analysts. Over time, the P&G team dedicated to the Walmart business grew to over 300 people globally, matched by a substantial increase in head count on the customer's side as well. And the business progressed, too, from $350 million to approximately $13 billion at its peak. Similar to the previous years, the partnership is cited in P&G's annual report as the largest customer relationship.

Looking back on the journey, Muccio stated:

> At peak times, P&G enjoyed a very close and trustful collaboration with Walmart, which corresponds to the five-star rating across the Triple Fit framework. During my time as leader of P&G global customer teams, we always tried to ensure that both sides were living up to the principle of "co-determination." In other words, no party would take a decision that could harm the other's position without prior consultation of the partner. A case in point were the notorious "Dear vendor . . ." letters, which we quickly eliminated, as they did not make sense in a five-star relationship anymore. Another shift was to advise Walmart on the best product portfolio neutrally, and not just make a hard sell on P&G's own products. We often ended up advising Walmart on how to deal with other suppliers in the best possible way. Sometimes, this was not beneficial to us but created a massive basis of trust. And last, we paid great attention to the principle of equality in our team culture. Irrespective of the hierarchy, all members of the team had the same small offices, and the corner offices were turned into meeting rooms. Such symbolic measures reinforced the teamwork culture and were also in line with the way Walmart's culture worked.[11]

In 2016–2017, however, the relationship started to decline, accompanied by some tough headlines in the business press.[12] One of the driving factors was the (temporary) elimination of the pioneering role in P&G's leadership team called the "President Walmart Team" from 2015 to 2018. Combined with increasing business pressure, the absence of the top role that we call the customer general manager or orchestrator led to more independent decisions in each company rather than the joint focus on issues that was the hallmark of the original team. The good news is that P&G recognized the importance of the relationship and reintroduced the customer GM role for Walmart in 2019. So, even if one would now question the value of one single and expensive orchestrator role at the company's top level, the symbolic measure of the action was priceless. The message was clear: this customer is equal to or even more important than products, so there is no room for individual agendas and suboptimal decisions. Eventually, P&G ended up with about a dozen five-star-type relationships that helped to grow and secure the top-customer business. In 2023, the top ten customers accounted for 40 percent of P&G's total net sales of $82 billion.[13]

We will focus in detail on the executive sponsor role in the next chapter and how it plays a critical role in Triple Fit strategy.

TAKEAWAYS

- Managing customer relationships happens in two modes—either the vendor or the orchestrator mode. Both have merits, but only the orchestrator will create value in the long run.

- Orchestrators create value way beyond the product-selling approach. They cover all parts of the business relationship as structured by the Triple Fit canvas and also provide commercial, knowledge, and leadership value.

- Companies should aspire to train and hire more salespeople that can grow into a customer general manager position. This will help them not only to create more value for customers but also to build bench strength for the talent pool of future business leaders.

REFLECTION QUESTIONS

- Where do you see yourself and your team—in the orchestrator or vendor roles? For further insights, visit triplefitstrategy.com.

- Which advantages of the orchestrator role do you need to deliver more of?

- How many customer general managers does your team have now? And how many will you need in the future?

CHAPTER 8

BUILD GROWTH CHAMPIONS

Some years ago, a top executive at a global chemical firm—we'll call him Robert—decided to meet with one of its major customers. He was new to the company and being unfamiliar with both the customer's challenges and his own firm's initiatives, he left a bad impression. Making matters worse, he offered to increase production capacity for the customer during spikes in demand, with no restrictions—a promise his firm couldn't keep. The customer account manager, Nadine, learned about the meeting and the promise only later, from one of her contacts at the customer company. The result: a relationship that remains badly damaged despite heroic repair efforts by Nadine and her team to live up to the poor promises made by the uninformed, unprepared executive.[1]

At about the same time, the pharmaceutical giant Merck decided to outsource its data-processing system. After evaluating proposals from several potential suppliers, the managers tasked with making the selection agreed: the contract should go to Accenture. But shortly before it was to be signed, Merck's CEO received a visit from Sam Palmisano, the CEO of IBM. Palmisano had risen through the ranks of IBM's sales force and had implemented the firm's integrated accounts program, which focused on core strategic customers. He fully understood the benefits of nurturing and leveraging executive-level relationships. Despite the manager's conviction in Accenture, Merck ultimately awarded the contract to IBM.[2]

Most executives see spending time with customers as part of their job and a way to stay abreast of the market. By engaging with the customers most critical to their firms' future, senior leaders at B2B suppliers can have a significant impact on their companies' revenue, profits, growth, shareholder value, and very survival. They often serve as executive sponsors for those key customer relationships. Overall, current research indicates that top management involvement with customers tends to be positive, but we suggest three important caveats:[3]

- CEO involvement as a persuader of last resort is not a sustainable approach. Even rock-star CEOs cannot routinely turn around closed (or almost closed) deals made with competitors.

- All top management team members face ongoing time constraints. They must carefully balance time allocated to customers with the demands of their core responsibilities—their day jobs.

- Top management–customer interactions frequently focus too much on securing immediate revenues rather than on long-run issues.[4]

Harvard researchers Michael Porter and Nitin Nohria recently found that CEOs spend roughly 70 percent of their time addressing internal constituents and only 3 percent with customers, less even than consultants and industry groups (5 percent each).[5] But as the opening examples of the chapter demonstrate, and as we have seen in our own research and consulting work with global sales organizations, the results of their involvement vary widely.

To study more closely the influence of CEOs and other leaders on sales, we searched for more hands-on evidence on top management with customers. In collaboration with Noel Capon from Columbia

Business School, Christoph found that top management engagement in customer affairs is not well studied.[6] Findings on top management relationships with customers were mostly anecdotal and do not offer practical advice.[7] And most importantly, hard evidence on the impact of top managers' customer interactions is largely missing.[8]

We continued the research by talking with top executives of B2B companies about their contacts with major customers. The vast majority reported extensive interactions and positive results. But when we interviewed the relevant account managers, we heard quite different stories. We realized that the executive interviews suffered from a strong self-reporting bias and that we needed to shift tactics. So we conducted 30 executive education workshops with 515 strategic and global account managers in New York, Rotterdam, St. Gallen (Switzerland), and Singapore over a period of six years. On the basis of that work, we identified five distinct roles that senior executives play in relation to strategic customers.

These roles connect to the nine Triple Fit building blocks because the presence of the right executive sponsors helps improve the relationship across all building blocks. It also enables the successful execution of a Triple Fit growth plan. Without the right executive sponsor support, the account teams are unable to orchestrate the planning, execution, and resource allocation in a customer-centric way. The executive sponsors are thus critical to all value-creation endeavors between a supplier and customer organization.

In the next sections, we discuss those roles, their rewards and risks, and the impact each has on business performance.

Types of Executive Involvement in Customer Relationships

In their interactions with customers, top executives have two core objectives: to increase revenue and to foster strong and enduring relationships. The five types of executive involvement yield different outcomes for those objectives. To be precise, we found four customer-focused roles plus one role where customer interaction was absent. Let's start with this one first.

Hands-off, or "not my problem"

It's not uncommon for senior executives to adopt a hands-off policy with their sales staffs: almost a third (28 percent) of those in our study did so. After all, they have their own responsibilities, competitive pressures and demands where they must do more with less. The CEO of one large manufacturing company told us, "I typically do not see customers. That's what the sales force is for. Our products and solutions are world class, and we have one of the strongest R&D groups in the industry. If only our account managers would do a better job of selling our value to customers!" Perhaps unsurprisingly, this executive is no longer with the organization, and a competitor has since acquired the firm.

But the motto "Let the sales force do its job" sounds eminently sensible. The human resources function should do its part, hiring the best talent to direct and manage the selling effort, and senior sales executives should ensure that salespeople have the tools and training to meet their goals. If results fall short, the remedy is clear: the sales team should make the appropriate process and personnel changes. "We don't expect top marketing and operations managers to get involved in finance," hands-off executives often tell us. "So why should any functional leader, much less the CEO, get involved in sales?" The assumption here is that all functions are equally important. But our work with companies around the world suggests that sales should be treated differently. Sales is a boundary role; it's the critical interface between supplier and customer.

Boundary-spanning positions are inherently stressful.[9] They are characterized by ambiguity and conflict over roles, work overload, and customer and ethical demands, so it's no surprise that executives often choose a hands-off role. Moreover, many senior managers mistakenly

FIGURE 8-1

Four active customer-engagement roles for senior leaders

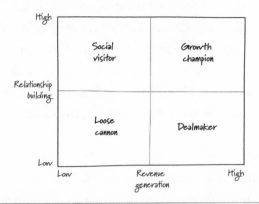

believe that they can't add much value to the selling effort, making the added stress of taking on a customer-facing role seem like a wasted investment of time. But as our example about IBM's Sam Palmisano demonstrates, they can indeed make a big difference—and a hands-off approach may represent missed opportunities. When the sales organization underperforms, revenue lags and everyone's budget suffers. When top managers give sales a boost, all functions benefit.

So what do leaders that are more actively involved in customer affairs do differently? They participate in some way in relationship building and revenue generation. Figure 8-1 gives an overview of the four active roles.

Loose cannon

A leader in this role typically meets with major customers without soliciting information or background from their account managers, who may not even know the meeting is happening (or, in the most egregious cases, that it has happened). Robert, the unprepared executive making impossible promises described earlier, is a classic example. Executives taking this approach—21 percent of those in our study—succeed at neither of the core goals. Their efforts rarely grow revenue, and they are more likely to damage than enhance the customer relationship. An account manager at a global technology-outsourcing firm told us, "I had been working my account for two years, gaining trust and making steady progress, and then it all fell apart. A corporate executive made an appointment with my customer's top management without letting me know and without any briefing or debriefing. He had no idea what was going on with the customer; the meeting set us back at least a year."

Account managers call such executives "seagulls." They fly in, make a lot of noise, leave a mess, and fly off. The senior sales executive at a major Canadian financial institution told us, "We don't have isolated seagulls; we have a whole flock of them!" If such interactions are so damaging, why are they so prevalent? Our workshops revealed that loose-cannon executives generally think they are being helpful; they see themselves as opening the doors to customers' executive suites. That's true in principle, but to actually be helpful, they need to forge strong working relationships with the account managers, enlisting their help in preparing for customer visits.

The good news is that most of the companies in our study that reported loose-cannon behavior also told us they were implementing processes to mitigate it, with reasonable success. The most effective approaches include strategic account management, whereby well-trained executives oversee critical customers; clear definition of roles and responsibilities and a process for briefing and debriefing executives for all customer visits, and an executive sponsor program for those who will be interfacing with major customers. Robert's firm learned an important lesson from his ill-fated visit: today its top executives are prohibited from visiting customers alone except under special circumstances and with proper engagement with account managers before and after meetings. The firm also put in place a central tracking system to ensure that no senior management visits are made without evaluating alternatives and to capture the results of all visits for use in future customer meetings.

Social visitor

Executives in this role—19 percent of those in our study—seek to build personal relationships with the customer rather than directly generate revenue. They focus on demonstrating their firm's commitment and creating trust. They specialize in meet-and-greets, often arranging educational events on the customer's premises, cocktail parties at trade shows, trips to marquee sporting events, and the like. The social visitor works the crowd but rarely delves into substantive discussions about business; indeed, spouses often attend the mostly social gatherings.

Although much less destructive than loose cannons, social visitors come with their own risks, and their impact ranges from mildly positive to mildly negative. Customers typically look forward to the planned events and leave with pleasant feelings, so the interactions generally do enhance personal relationships. But if customers perceive that executives are interested only in schmoozing or in posing for a photo at the signing of a big deal, they may become frustrated by the lack of depth in the relationship—especially if competitors are engaging with them on a more meaningful level.

The CEO of a Europe-based engineering firm frequently met with customers at trade shows and social events. After some time, he accepted an invitation to visit one customer's US headquarters—on the face of it, a useful move. Although he advised the account manager of the visit, he decided to make the trip alone. The customer's CEO, accustomed to productive visits from high-performing suppliers, awaited him with an entourage of innovation leaders, logistics experts, and purchasing managers in tow. Clearly surprised, he said to his visitor, "Good to see you, but where on earth is your account manager and her team?" For this customer CEO, as for many others we have spoken with, a purely social relationship, without the participation of the account manager, was not enough.

And if treated too casually, a social-visitor approach can quickly turn into a loose-cannon situation. One supplier in the beverage industry had enjoyed a long-term relationship with an important customer when a new executive sponsor came on board. The account manager scheduled an introductory meeting with the customer's top management. But the executive sponsor postponed the meeting three times, citing minor reasons. In frustration, the customer turned to a more attentive competitor and opened discussions on next-generation packaging design, resulting in a huge revenue loss for the supplier.

Dealmaker

Executives in this role are highly focused on revenue and only marginally concerned with relationship building. In our study, 18 percent of executives fell into this group. Sam Palmisano represents an extreme form of dealmaking behavior; so let's look at a more typical example.

A global coating-systems manufacturer had contracted to supply eco-friendly, cost-saving production technology to a leading German automotive firm. Although the technology had performed well in laboratory and field tests, the supplier could not stabilize it on the customer's main production line, and the contractually agreed-on time frame for implementation was coming to an end. So after speaking with the account manager, the supplier's CEO visited both the customer's headquarters and the production facility and secured an extension. With the extra time gained, his firm was able to solve the problem on-site, and the deal was rescued.

Such engagement may be necessary to close a deal. When a customer is considering whether to sign a contract, the make-or-break issue is often not the value proposition offered by the account manager but whether the supplier is likely to live up to its commitments. An account manager's promises are of limited reassurance; only a senior executive, and sometimes only the CEO, can fully commit the firm's resources. The same is often true of customers making buying decisions: middle managers negotiate deals and make recommendations, but senior managers have the final word on which supplier to choose. (Recall how Merck's CEO overruled his advisers in signing with IBM.) We have observed cases in which a customer's top manager intervened in the buying process and reversed a middle manager's decision, even accepting penalties to void a signed contract with an unwanted supplier.

But the dealmaker approach, too, comes with risks. If negotiations are frequently escalated to the executive suite, upward delegation may become the norm—an unsustainable way of doing business. And while the senior executive team can certainly be invaluable in closing especially sticky or crucial deals, customers may become frustrated by numerous requests for rush meetings.

To master the dealmaker role, internal coordination is crucial. Yet with their focus on revenue rather than relationships, dealmakers may neglect communication with key players in their own companies, sometimes leading to costly mistakes. At a global manufacturer of materials for the paint industry, the dealmaker of one business unit terminated an R&D project being conducted in collaboration with a customer because he deemed the potential revenue— €300,000—to be insufficient. In doing so, he failed to consider the €20 million in revenue the project was expected to generate for a sister business unit.

A dealmaker must stay in constant communication with account managers and protect their role in the process. In their zeal to secure business, dealmakers sometimes go overboard in offering concessions. If customers suspect that deeper discounts are available from higher-ranking executives, they may bypass their account managers or demand that the dealmakers be involved in every negotiation. Consider the extreme measures one account manager resorted to when his division president decided to accompany him to close an important deal. "Shortly after the meeting started, the customer pushed for significant price reductions," the account manager told us. "The division president was so focused on winning the deal that he was about to agree—which would have cost us more than $2 million in profits. I didn't know how to stop him, so I faked a heart attack. The meeting ended, and a few weeks later I negotiated a much better price."[10]

Growth champion

This role demonstrates the most productive customer-facing behavior. Leaders in this group have a keen focus on both relationships and revenue building, and as they unlock growth opportunities, they serve as role models for others in the organization. Unfortunately, the smallest share of executives in our study—just 14 percent—fit this profile.

John Chambers, the CEO of Cisco for many years, was a growth champion for the company. He had learned the ropes of customer interaction as a sales rep at IBM and was Cisco's senior vice president of worldwide sales and operations before taking the helm. He frequently accompanied account managers on client visits and would solicit immediate feedback on what he could do better to enhance the value he offered to customers. He also leveraged the firm's technology to interact with customers virtually, long before Covid-19 made videoconference calls commonplace.

To be effective growth champions, supplier executives must become directly involved with strategic customers over and above the demands of their day jobs, and they must adopt the customer's perspective, even attending customer strategy sessions. Growth champions support processes aimed at improving business performance, such as the use of customer profitability metrics and best-practice systems. Perhaps most important, they pave the way for cultural change: others in the organization model their behavior on that of growth champions, often becoming more customer-centric themselves.

Growth champions are willing to break internal barriers (and sometimes actual rules) in their pursuit of long-term customer success. In a significant downsizing, IBM laid off an experienced engineer who had provided critical tech support to a key account. The account manager realized that losing this team member would severely weaken IBM's position with the customer, so he contacted his "partnership executive," IBM's term for executive sponsor. The PE could not undo the layoff, but he agreed to retain the engineer as a consultant and secured the necessary funding. The engineer served in that capacity for a dozen years, boosting the revenue from several strategic customers.

FIGURE 8-2

Executive sponsor roles and Triple Fit focus

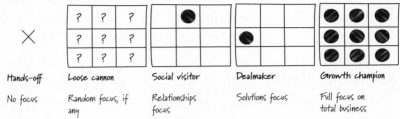

Hands-off	Loose cannon	Social visitor	Dealmaker	Growth champion
No focus	Random focus, if any	Relationships focus	Solutions focus	Full focus on total business

However, growth champions, too, have their downsides: They can be prone to patronizing behavior and micromanagement, especially if they were once sales executives or account managers themselves. A top executive at a Japanese IT firm was enthusiastic about supporting a particular customer's account manager and his team, scheduling weekly calls to monitor progress and drive growth. These actions put immense pressure on the account manager, who told us, only partly in jest, "It's all well and good to have such a committed executive, but I always look forward to when he's on vacation!"

Looking at the activity focus of the five roles, we found an interesting correlation. The two negative roles, hands-off and loose cannon, were not focusing on Triple Fit topics. The main reason for their action (or inaction) was simply a random incident or well-intended but badly executed intervention like, for example, the unrealistic promise made in the opening case of this chapter. When we looked at the activity focus of the three other roles, we started to see some sort of partial or even full focus on the Triple Fit logic. Figure 8-2 summarizes the role focus and its connection to the Triple Fit perspective.

Finding the Right Roles

After identifying the five types of top management involvement and their connection to the Triple Fit canvas, we also sought to understand how each affects financial performance. We compiled five-year growth rates for sales and profits for each company in our study, drawing on SEC filings and other publicly accessible databases. A CEO's style in dealing with customers is just one variable that affects growth, of course, but among firms with hands-off and loose-cannon executives, both sales and profits were generally flat. Social visitors and dealmakers delivered growth rates that were, on average, two to three times those of their hands-off and loose-cannon counterparts— and growth champions drove growth at twice the rate of social visitors and dealmakers, making them far and away the most effective group (see figure 8-3).

Does this mean that every high-level executive should act as a growth champion in every interaction with a major customer? Not necessarily. Suppliers should build growth-champion roles for strategic customers whenever feasible, but if a customer resists such collaboration, the supplier executive should adopt a dealmaker or a social-visitor role and focus on executing it to the fullest extent possible.

Supplier executives should take context into account before deciding on their approach. They should consider each customer's behavior, the importance of the customer to the supplier and vice versa, and the characteristics of the customer's buying process. If a customer

FIGURE 8-3

Performance effects across the four types of active interactions with customers

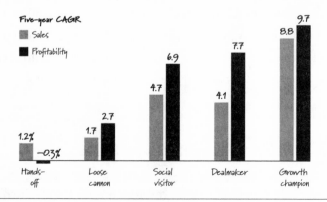

conducts itself in a purely transactional manner, investing in a growth-champion relationship may indeed be a waste of resources; a dealmaker—even one at a lower organizational level—might obtain equally good or better outcomes in the short term. Certain customers may lend themselves to a more opportunistic approach using social visitors. But over the long term, most suppliers will benefit from moving their customer relationships to the next level. Some of the most successful executives we know began their customer-interaction journeys as social visitors or dealmakers, eventually evolving into growth champions. We have worked with others who assume the growth-champion role for their most important customer relationships while remaining social visitors or dealmakers with others.

The bottom line is that CEOs who eschew the growth-champion role with strategic customers are putting their companies at a disadvantage. If a customer seeks collaborative engagement beyond social-visitor or dealmaker discussions and the supplier fails to step up, the customer may well turn to a competitor to shape its future.

What Makes a Growth Champion?

On the basis of our research, we've sketched a profile of essential traits, which organizations can use to spot such leaders in their ranks.[11]

- Compatibility: Achieves a close personal fit with both customer executives and the account manager

- Availability: Is responsive to customers and the account manager and sales team; no excuses

- Initiative: Is willing to go above and beyond, to adopt the customer's perspective, and to break internal barriers in the service of long-term customer success

- Knowledge: Has an in-depth understanding of the firm's and the customer's strategy and capabilities

- Communication skills: Can speak the language of the customer, sales teams, and functional experts

- People skills: Is committed to strong teamwork, coaching, and listening

- Results orientation: Has a history and track record of meeting or exceeding objectives

Using Triple Fit Strategy to Be a Growth Champion

We recommend that while doing the Triple Fit process, companies conduct an annual review of each strategic customer relationship and assign growth champions according to long-term business potential rather than current buying behavior. Executive team members must venture outside their comfort zones to assume unfamiliar responsibilities—and help managers throughout their companies do the same. Consider Henkel, a German-based consumer packaged goods manufacturer that was locked in tough competition with Procter & Gamble and Unilever. Its siloed brand strategy limited its ability to interact with customers across its full product portfolio. So shortly after becoming CEO, Kasper Rørsted instituted a "meet the customer" program for top managers across all brands. He also launched a competition among senior executives, tracking their customer-focused activities. Customer-interaction reports soon became a regular item on the agenda of management meetings, and senior executive visits to customers dramatically increased in number and effectiveness. In turn, customer relationships were supported by the Triple Fit methodology, yielding better growth results than the relationships without Triple Fit focus.[12]

Supplier companies should also have an executive sponsor program to enable a successful execution of the Triple Fit value-creation process. These programs can take many different shapes: some are highly structured and metrics-driven; others are informal arrangements between top managers and the sales organization. But the most effective programs have certain assumptions in common. They recognize that executive sponsorship is a priority, not an optional activity; that sponsors should commit to two- to three-year assignments to ensure consistency and depth; and that sponsors are not the owners of the customer relationship and must consult with account managers before and after customer visits. Such programs should not be set in stone; they should be evaluated and adjusted as customer needs or the supplier's own priorities evolve. For example, centralized management and coordination of a sponsorship program may become more important as a small supplier grows to a midsize or large enterprise and its relationship management issues multiply in complexity and number.

Surveying our 515 workshop participants, we learned that companies with an executive sponsor program had a significantly higher share of growth champions among their top managers (26 percent) than did firms without such a sponsor program (just 4 percent). They also reported a heightened awareness of the importance of top management involvement in customer interactions and a more systematic approach for strategically applying the most effective executive roles.

After this study, we further tested and applied the findings at midsize and small firms from different industries where we saw quite a few real-life growth champions in action.

Consider, for example, the case of Sorec, a recycling company based in St. Gallen, Switzerland. A family-owned business for seventy years with strong connections to local companies and authorities, Sorec set out for the next chapter of its history. After a conversation with us, Christoph Solenthaler, one of the company's two owners, decided to apply the Triple Fit canvas to selected existing (and new) business relationships. In less than one year, Sorec was able to identify real customer priorities beyond obvious pain points and win new business with customers that were previously considered too large to handle. One case in point is a recent cooperation with Canon for the profitable recycling of toner cartridges. The collaborative approach of the negotiation enabled Sorec to integrate a brand-new innovation directly into the value chain of their partner Canon, leading to significant commercial benefits including a higher market share of 15 percent and industry legitimization. During a Triple Fit strategy workshop, Canon stated that they valued the structured discussion more than anything else, as it focused on their business priorities, not Sorec's. The lesson from this case: even if your company is a small player in a big market, one growth champion who runs a strategic dialogue based on the Triple Fit canvas can make a significant difference.

Another growth champion at the helm of a large corporation is Maersk's CEO Vincent Clerc, as we learned in chapter 1. Not to our credit, but to the credit of the involved Maersk frontline sales teams and decision-makers, we can report that a lot has happened since Clerc initiated the Triple Fit pilot initiative in 2019. Today, Triple Fit has found its way into the organization in many ways, becoming a core part of Clerc's toolbox as a growth champion. For example, Maersk's account plans for important customers also consist of a Triple Fit canvas. Updated quarterly, these account plans have started turning from mere wish lists to jointly created growth plans that exceed the expectations on both sides. And executive sponsor briefings are now being given based on one-page, customer-validated Triple Fit canvas presentations, thus making the best use of the busy schedules of everyone. Twice per year, Maersk invites customers to global or regional advisory board meetings to discuss how both sides can further shape the future. And once per year, Maersk hosts an internal meeting for all executive sponsors, where they discuss insights from Triple Fit–powered relationships and develop conclusions for the future work of executive sponsors in the growth-champion mode. The lesson from this case: larger companies need more structure in the executive sponsor approach but will benefit greatly from the larger number of growth champions that, in turn, create a massive differentiator from competition.

A final caveat: companies should bear in mind that not all senior executives make good executive sponsors. That's why some companies we worked together with, recognized the importance of a strong match; the account managers could request a different executive sponsor if the dynamic was not working well, as long as they could cite a solid reason for the request.

Top management involvement in B2B customer relationships can pay enormous dividends for suppliers and their customers. One of our workshop participants summed up the challenge succinctly. "It's the responsibility of account managers and their teams to manage the customer's share of wallet," he told us. "The role of senior management is to win the customer's mind." Becoming more customer-centric is not just another project for top executives to put on the to-do list; it is an essential part of growth and a fundamental driver of success.[13]

TAKEAWAYS

- By directly engaging with customers, senior leaders can have a significant impact on their company's revenue, profits, growth, stakeholder value, and survival. But the results vary widely.

- Senior leaders play five distinct roles in relation to customers, depending on the degree to which they prioritize relationship building and revenue generation. Some take a hands-off approach, while others are loose cannons, social visitors, dealmakers, or growth champions.

- Leaders who want to best support their teams' Triple Fit journeys should strive to be growth champions for core customers whenever possible and stay in this role for multiple years. An annual review of these engagements is highly advisable.

REFLECTION QUESTIONS

- Where do you see you or your executive sponsors in the executive engagement matrix? To download a free assessment, go to triplefitstrategy.com.

- If you could double the current number of growth champions in your company, how much would your business grow?

- How many growth champions can you currently identify on the customer side? How could you develop better relationships with them to garner their support?

CHAPTER 9

ESTABLISH A ONE-COMPANY CULTURE

A few years ago, we worked with a global IT solutions provider we call Navigator. The task was to implement a sales growth program, focusing on value creation for and together with the most promising customers. One of the toughest customers at that time was a soft-drink giant we will call Peppermint. The internal Triple Fit analysis revealed that Navigator did business with Peppermint in an uncoordinated way. So, Navigator sent a team to study the soft-drink maker's overall business setup and come up with proposals to make it more competitive. After a meeting with Peppermint's chief information officer, numerous ideas for closer cooperation were adopted. Navigator requested a three-day Triple Fit workshop to be held at Peppermint's US headquarters. Both companies delegated about a dozen people each to work in full depth on a future more-value-creation-oriented strategy. After the top brass of both firms kicked off the workshop, the working teams created a list of Peppermint's likely future information-technology needs, helping the company avoid purchases of equipment and software licenses that it might not need or that might be too costly. Navigator also showed where it could relieve the company in terms of IT management, not a core competence for the client, thus increasing efficiency. At the end of the three days, the results were presented to the stakeholders and approved.

Since then, Navigator's business with the customer has grown ten-fold in less than three years. And Peppermint received more business from Navigator as well, increasing the soft-drink maker's presence at Navigator's employee catering locations, for example. On a larger scale, Navigator, tripled its international sales volume and cut customer management program costs by more than 50 percent in the first five years that it adopted Triple Fit. Senior managers at Navigator also stayed closely involved with the initiative, helping to focus customer dialogue not just on operational issues but on how to shape the future together. Navigator's executive board members, meanwhile, annually review the company's top-fifty account plans to support joint business development.

Connecting the "One Company" Dots

Navigator's experience with Peppermint demonstrates one powerful lesson: the best-prepared sales teams work with their customers using a one-company mindset to unlock new sources of value. Triple Fit strategy not only helps companies determine where they are struggling or needing transformation, but also helps them identify valuable opportunities for future innovation and growth together with their customers. But across our sample of nearly ten thousand cases, less than 10 percent are there. More than 90 percent are still in the product-selling mode; thus, they are not exploiting the growth potential they could tap into if they would change to a broader-focused value-creation mode.[1]

From our own work in more than one thousand Triple Fit implementation projects, we can conclude that the first step to master the transition from product selling to value creation at a company level is to connect the dots on both sides. Especially in the post-Covid-19 era, it has become more important for organizations to be aware of their greater purpose and identity and how they choose to work and grow together with their customers. The current era is one of un-precedented connectivity through technology, shifting demograph-ics in terms of markets, and new levels of speed, simplicity, and agility that requires organizations to innovate and learn faster than ever, and fundamental shifts around organizational structures that require greater flexibility including the new work trends that are here to stay.[2] It is clear to us that organizations cannot go through these transforma-tional changes alone if they want to be future ready with new business models that sustain and create growth; they need to do that with their customers.

A sales leader once candidly stated during one of our implemen-tation projects: "Any given organization at any given time is going through one or the other transformation or change management ini-tiative, including my own organization and my customer's organiza-tion. If I can tap into a greater understanding of this, we can really help each other and find common ground for value creation." This led us to reflect on the topic of change and how it needs to unfold in a com-pany to be truly effective. Given the huge investments and commit-ments across all levels that companies put into dealing with change both externally and internally, it merits a deeper understanding of why and how a company needs to make change management deci-sions, and what to do to make the changes stick.

Under the umbrella term of "transformation initiatives," every company strives to reach the next level of growth and performance through them. On the upside, most change efforts look encourag-ing as they aim to strengthen business processes, encourage cross-functional teams, and focus on innovation to deliver better offerings to customers. But not far away are the cost management change ini-tiatives focused on restructuring efforts—redefining the company's myriad departments with its dark side of employee layoffs.

In his classic book *Leading Change: Why Transformation Efforts Fail*, John P. Kotter wrote,

> Over the past decade, I have watched more than 100 companies try to remake themselves into significantly better competitors.

They have included large organizations (Ford) and small ones (Landmark Communications), companies based in the United States (General Motors) and elsewhere (British Airways), corporations that were on their knees (Eastern Airlines), and companies that were earning good money (Bristol-Myers Squibb). These efforts have gone under many banners: total quality management, reengineering, right sizing, restructuring, cultural change, and turnaround. But, in almost every case, the basic goal has been the same: to make fundamental changes in how business is conducted to help cope with a new, more challenging market environment. A few of these corporate change efforts have been very successful. A few have been utter failures. Most fall somewhere in between, with a distinct tilt toward the lower end of the scale.[3]

In our research, we have observed that one of the key reasons these change efforts are not successful is because they are not focused on transforming the right things in the first place. Most of them are defined based on the inside-out or product-centric perspective, rather than the outside-in or customer-centric perspective. Improving the company's competitive advantage, finding new markets, keeping up with the technology and innovation trends, and ensuring that the financial performance is on a growth trajectory are all valid concerns. Add economic or industry threats or even well-timed opportunities to the mix, and these external factors create increasing urgency to position a company for success.

The proverbial saying, "Culture eats strategy for breakfast," sums up the importance and the challenge of changing an organizational culture to make growth happen.[4] However, this is much more than having an ideal organizational setup or an employee-centric culture that is aligned for growth. Traditionally, growth has been the domain of sales teams, without giving them always their rightful place in the organization, including B2B sales, which has only recently progressed to become a strategic function in most organizations. Sales has long been considered the push part of marketing, where salespeople are expected to ensure that what the product teams have carefully designed and the marketing teams have meticulously packaged is sold in the market. However, this product-centric mindset has long outlived its utility, and there's a greater need to understand customers and make sure that understanding is filtered to all departments, including marketing and product teams. Even with strategy, sales is the reality check of strategy execution because a good strategy is about doing the things that really matter to your customers and that surpass the competition in terms of the value created.

And yet, sales, marketing, product teams, and the strategy function talking to each other is not enough if they do not talk about the right things, such as servicing the customers together. Collaboration for the sake of collaboration and breaking silos to exchange information isn't a long-term solution if there is no innovation road map or joint commitment with the company's most strategic customers to bring products to market. Collaboration among the different functions is just not a means to an end; it is crucial to have a one-company mindset in serving the customers as a united organization. This is where the focus on important customers comes into play: to ensure that the voice of the customer reaches all the departments, and the right teams are in place to drive the changes that address the obstacles as well as the opportunities for growth. This is what driving growth based on customer-centricity truly means, instead of continuing to do what the organization has been doing before.

Our research shows that a one-company mindset is likely to succeed when it is in line with the company's overall vision, strategy, and value-creation focus. In practice, however, it can be difficult to get this to work between functions or even business units, especially for a large global organization with a decentralized structure, where all the departments have their own agendas, and the business units are seeking to maximize their own profit-and-loss statements. While senior management at the headquarters of this large global firm would want to make customer-centric investment decisions in order to outpace competition, it wants the different functions and business units to cooperate to fuel this growth together with the customer-facing sales teams.

The challenge is that the organization isn't yet functioning as one company internally, because each of the functional heads and business unit leaders have established their own cultures with the autonomy that a decentralized organizational structure allows for, without necessarily putting the customer first.[5] Senior management at the headquarters creates a list of strategic priorities that ends up being handed down to business units. This is where a unified, organizational, one-company culture needs to come into play because if not understood and worked with as an untapped force, a fragmented culture will absolutely eat strategy for breakfast, lunch, and dinner, creating impediments to the execution of the organization's overall strategic focus.

In our work supporting customer-centricity efforts at a range of global organizations, we've seen this scenario play out again and again. It doesn't have to, however. Companies can achieve a one-company culture across their business functions and decentralized business units—if senior management takes the time to identify and commit to a one-company vision based on a customer-validated Triple Fit strategy and then implements the road map for each function and business unit to achieve it.

The Triple Fit strategy must begin with customers first and involves asking the most important questions that will drive the organization to be ready for the future together with the customers. The companies that embrace this value-creation mindset tend to realize quicker decision-making by stakeholders; greater operational agility in terms of planning, execution, and resource allocation; and stronger buy-in and engagement from regional teams—usually resulting in better overall performance while tapping into customer-centric growth.

One of the key causes of conflict between different functions is the inside-out versus outside-in focus of the departments. For example, consider an internal product development team and a key account management team within any large organization. The product development team is likely focused on making the products better in terms of innovation and quality, for instance, but not necessarily through customer-validated inputs. This creates an inside-out focus. The key account management team, by contrast, is speaking to the customers and focused on fast-changing market and industry trends that might require completely different products in the future, creating an outside-in focus. The organization will end up working with conflicting objectives if these teams start to focus in separate directions, thereby slowing down their own implementation timelines. This is what silos look like in action, and it eventually creates further blockages in supply chains or knowledge sharing once other departments are added to the mix. Before we know it, the entire organization is at a crossroad of strategic priorities and resource-allocation decisions. There isn't the focus on customer-led change initiatives and development of capabilities that the customers are asking for, leading the company to miss significant growth opportunities in good times and secure its existing business in bad times.

Here's the brutal truth we have observed across industries: if the organization isn't aligned with what the strategic customers really want, no internal initiative or overall strategy execution can go far or last long. If revenue streams dry up or don't end up in a growth cycle, all inside-out efforts are a waste of time and resources. The way to avoid this is for the top management to ensure that a one-company culture focused on customers exists in the entire organization and drives the right actions across functions and business units.

The reason organizations can effectively plan, execute, and implement a value-creation focus with their customers based on Triple Fit strategy is because the nine building blocks consider different perspectives from functions and business units, ensuring that any transformation effort to be future ready begins internally as a one-company culture. In the previous two chapters, we saw that when sales executives and customer-facing teams evolve into the role of customer general managers and their management teams and executive sponsors evolve into the role of growth champions, the very fabric of an organization changes. In addition, once they start talking to their leadership and functional teams along with the business units, it creates a momentum effect of making sure that every department is aware of the customer-led strategic priorities and vice versa—the customers know what the organization stands by as a single entity. This is because the different organizations, teams, entities, and units are integrated behind each of the building blocks as follows:

- Strategies: Corporate strategy team

- Relationships: C-level teams and executive sponsors

- Communication: Communications team

- Solutions: Product and marketing teams

- Processes: Operations and procurement teams

- Systems: IT, legal, finance, CRM, and HR teams

- People: Sales and account management team

- Structures: Business units and country heads

- Knowledge: R&D and innovation team

There's no reason why even a heavily siloed company determined to shift the responsibilities in a decentralized way can't achieve customer-centric growth. But the sales executives and business leaders must ensure that all functions and business units are on board and attempt to create an environment in which each team feels empowered. This works when there are lighthouse cases for strategic customers where the entire organization has successfully worked as one company to deliver growth and can share the Triple Fit best practices. Using the Triple Fit canvas to map the different company

FIGURE 9-1

The one-company view through the Triple Fit lens

	Strategies	Relationships	Communication
Planning fit	Corporate strategy team	C-level executive sponsors	Communications team
Execution fit	Solutions Product and marketing teams	Processes Operations and procurement teams	Systems IT, finance, legal, CRM, and HR teams
Resources fit	People Account management team	Structures Business units / country heads	Knowledge R&D team

functions and connect the dots between internal functions is an important step toward a one-company culture. Triple Fit itself connects the silos (see figure 9-1).

Avoiding One-Company Traps

After connecting the dots internally, a successful transformation effort requires the company's leadership to cooperate with its most important B2B customers to ensure that the guiding principles behind shaping the change efforts have a solid foundation. Because change management is hard and customer-centricity is a huge mission for any organization, no matter what its size, the direction of any companywide transformation must be decided with the customers on board. We have found that defining the change efforts based on the proper application of the guiding principles of Triple Fit will make all the difference. This, in turn, will lead to a one-company mindset in their planning and execution, thereby setting the organization on the right course and navigating through the obstacles with course-correcting actions together with the customers.

To recapitulate, the three Triple Fit guiding principles for a one-company mindset are:

- Realigning the strategy and transformation focus to customer-centric planning

- Reconfiguring the solutions design and their execution with customer-validated inputs

- Reallocating organizational resources for mutual success with customer commitments

Taking these principles forward, however, we have seen that it's not enough to apply only one or two as considered appropriate. Even though it may sound like a one-size-fits-all call, we can confirm that only the simultaneous application of all three principles will help companies master the transition from product-centricity to customer-centricity and, hence, the transition toward a one-company mindset. Even if there is good Triple Fit performance at one or two Triple Fit levels, low performance in the (missing) third level can sabotage the whole implementation plan. Figure 9-2 summarizes the three most common traps that companies can fall into. Let's have a look at each trap in more detail.

FIGURE 9-2

The Triple Fit guiding principles and their associated traps

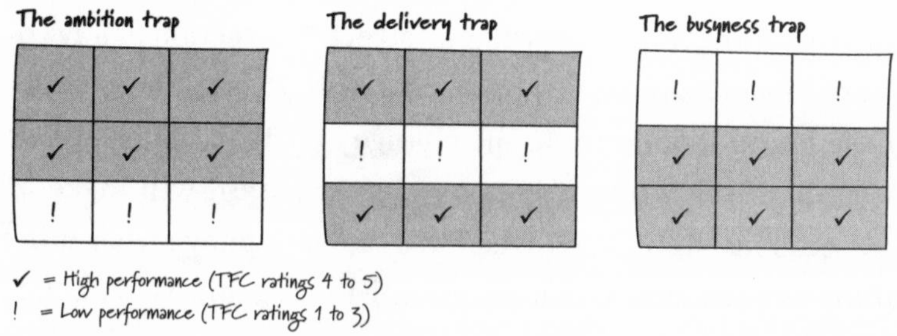

✓ = High performance (TFC ratings 4 to 5)
! = Low performance (TFC ratings 1 to 3)

The ambition trap

In the ambition trap, companies show consolidated high Triple Fit scores. The Triple Fit scores should reflect a combined view from all relevant customers—similar to the hot-issues perspective featured in chapter 3. The challenge of this pattern is that while the planning fit and the execution fit seem to match customer expectations, the same is not true for the resources fit. Consequently, companies get stuck in what we call the "ambition trap"—lots of ideas and commitments from both sides, but no adequate resources allocation, staffing, or investments made to create a breakthrough in joint value creation. A case in point is the experience of an information technology services company we call ITS. After a first Triple Fit initiative, ITS made good progress in aligning its ambitions with clients, at both the local and international levels. But when it came to fueling the execution via shifted resource allocation, the initiative started to run out of steam, as the ITS team members were not adequately trained or freed from other tasks in existing local country structures; knowledge development and sharing was not possible due to conflicting, more important priorities. Consequently, ITS started to miss several important business trends and opportunities—a scenario that it could have avoided.

The delivery trap

In the delivery trap, companies show consolidated high Triple Fit scores at the planning and resources fit levels. The Triple Fit scores should reflect a combined view from all relevant customers, similar to the hot-issues perspective in chapter 3. In this pattern, the planning fit and the resources fit seem to meet customer expectations, the same is not true for the execution fit. As a result, companies get stuck in what we call the "delivery trap"—lots of ideas and commitments from both sides, but no ability to deliver on the promises and execute great value creation ideas, despite available funding and further resource support. Consider, for example, the case of a health insurance company we call Subsidium. Acknowledging the historically difficult relationships with hospitals, Subsidium's management launched a Triple Fit pilot project with selected hospitals across its home country. The Triple Fit ratings indicated strengths at the planning fit and resources fit levels. But the execution efforts were stuck in the delivery trap, and for eighteen months there was a back-and-forth between both organizations' operations teams accusing each other of sabotage. Only when the Subsidium CEO, together with key personnel from the hospitals, personally intervened and organized roundtables for stakeholders from both sides, did the company find its way out of the trap.

The busyness trap

In the busyness trap, the consolidated Triple Fit ratings look good for the execution fit and the resources fit. But the company is not aligned and connected well enough with its customers in terms of strategies, relationships, and communication. The resulting trap is "busyness," and instead of focusing on strategic business issues as identified and validated together with its clients, the company does just more of the same and falls into what we call the busyness trap.[6] A case in point is the experience of a tier-one supplier to the automotive industry we call CarTec. When CarTec was confronted by the procurement departments of its largest clients with cost savings beyond regular discount requests, it doubled its efforts to find efficiencies in its execution efforts and resource allocation, with disappointing results. In other words, CarTec accelerated its internal efforts without proper alignment to customer strategies and became increasingly busy with internal issues, finally leading to the loss of key contracts with several of its fifteen key accounts. An analysis of Triple Fit hot issues revealed later that CarTec could have avoided this loss, if it had engaged in a strategic dialogue with its key accounts up-front and had focused on validated top customer priorities.

If your Triple Fit ratings for the hot issues ever show one of these patterns, it is time to close the gaps at the lowest-performing level and not to wait until it is too late. The good news is that these are consolidated results. So, most likely, there is a spread of examples pointing to already existing good practices in a relationship that could be replicated for all others.

Transforming to One-Company Behavior

Maersk had its aha moments when it dealt with connecting the dots and identified potential one-company traps. Reviewing the results of the Triple Fit pilot phase that had started in 2019, Maersk's CEO, Vincent Clerc, initiated the first Triple Fit pilot project in 2019. Reviewing the results of the Triple Fit pilot phase three years later, Clerc and his management team concluded that there was enough positive evidence to continue. Think, for example, of the previously described case (in chapter 2) of Christine Dickson, the Maersk key client director who orchestrated the business with her customer Elegance for mutual benefits, or the ahead-of-time contract renewal with a record business volume orchestrated by Moshe Loberant for Maersk and its customer Kotahi-Fonterra (chapter 1).

With the ambition to build the most customer-centric logistics firm in the entire industry, in 2022 Clerc tasked Sanjay Vasudevan, Maersk's global head of key account management and sustainability, to drive growth with its most valuable customers above market and company growth rates. To gain a comprehensive picture, Vasudevan started to look at Triple Fit results but not only at the single customer relationship but at the customer portfolio level. Pooling the results of all the Triple Fit canvases jointly developed with customers, Maersk developed insights into strategic customer priorities above its many industry verticals. Deep dives into the booster zone matrix (see chapter 4) revealed that many customers were following a healthy growth path, while others required more attention and measures to protect or optimize the collaboration.

The consolidated Triple Fit hot-issues ratings from a pool of more than fifty global clients also showed that Maersk was about to fall into the delivery trap. In concrete terms, the ratings for the execution fit were the lowest across all nine building blocks. But since Triple Fit ratings are leading indicators, it was not too late to correct the course. So Vasudevan initiated a multistep plan to establish a one-company culture along the motto "What if we and our clients were one company?" The following pillars illustrate Vasudevan's strategic priorities:

- Train all global client directors to orchestrate value creation with key clients

- Involve customers in a strategic dialogue via newly formed customer advisory boards

- Enhance existing account plans with the Triple Fit framework validated by customers

- Enable Maersk's senior managers to act as executive sponsors in growth champion mode

- Cascade the value-creation training to the next set of client managers

Today, Triple Fit has found its way into the organization in many ways. For example, Maersk's account plans for important customers consist of a customer-validated Triple Fit canvas. Updated quarterly, these account plans have started turning from mere wish lists to jointly created growth plans that exceed expectations on both sides. And executive sponsor briefings are now being given based on one-page, customer-validated Triple Fit canvas presentations, thus making the best use of the busy schedules of everyone. And once per year, Maersk invites customers to global or regional advisory board meetings to discuss how both sides can further shape the future. With these actions, Maersk can connect the dots not only internally, but also externally, and create alignment between and across functions (see figure 9-1).

At the time of our writing, in 2024, Vasudevan is rolling out the Triple Fit framework to all of Maersk's global customers and cascading the approach to additional customers in local markets.

FIGURE 9-3

Maersk's transformation journey results between 2019 and 2023

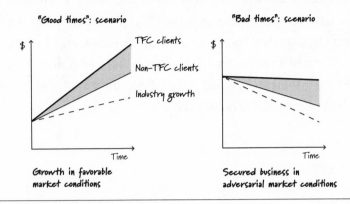

Consequently, Maersk has seen above-average results despite the logistics market slowdown after the extraordinarily high profits made during the Covid-19 pandemic. The results of Maersk's Triple Fit initiative fall into two distinct scenarios: on the one hand, Maersk experienced double-digit growth under favorable market conditions for those customers that were using the Triple Fit canvas. On the other hand, Maersk experienced stable business from Triple Fit accounts compared to the sharp declines of many others even during the most recent downturns. Figure 9-3 illustrates the logic of both scenarios.

. . .

Organization culture is not something that should exist only as motivational slogans for employees and corporate taglines in email signatures.[7] A strong one-company mindset with well-defined ways of collaboration between all functions and teams is critical to creating a cohesive and successful organization and making it truly customer-centric in the long run. Culture is what ultimately gives an organization its competitive advantage, because it is extremely hard to replicate and is ultimately unique to each organization.[8] Cutting through price wars, Triple Fit strategy drives profitable growth, *and* makes the world a better place. When leaders choose—and build—the kind of Triple Fit culture they want the organization to embody, they create a virtuous cycle, attracting the right people that will thrive in their company, unlock their value-creation focus, and turbocharge the overall performance. We hope that for all companies large and small, Triple Fit strategy creates a lasting impact on the way businesses thrive over the years to come.

TAKEAWAYS

- A simple question, "What if we were one company?" can change the game, one relationship at a time.

- Focus is not enough. To avoid the one-company traps, you need to consider the big picture that consolidates all three fit levels either at a single relationship level or a portfolio of relationships and act accordingly.

- Triple Fit canvas insights are early warning systems to build better business relationships and a more customer-centric organization.

REFLECTION QUESTIONS

- If your customer relationships would really live up to the principle of one company, how many examples of growth increasing ten times would you have?

- Which of the three one-company traps do you observe in your organization? To take a self-assessment quiz for your company, go to triplefitstrategy.com.

- Which functions and departments would need to be aligned to overcome these traps?

A FINAL THOUGHT

Often we are asked for advice on how to start building lasting customer relationships and boost growth without a large budget for external help. Here's our answer:

First, create a total business view by analyzing one or several business relationships with the Triple Fit canvas. Although this may not feel like an exact science, ensure that both sides understand each other's perceived reality and discuss the results. Then, focus on mutually agreed hot issues and define a realistic, broader joint vision, and clear goals and objectives.

Second, understand the internal politics. Find those stakeholders on both sides who will support your case, as it ideally will also advance their career. Then, identify and realize low-hanging fruits to achieve quick wins and prove your case in ninety days. Don't expect instant miracles, but plan for the long game by helping each other, for example, by training key people regularly or sharing helpful information.

And third, foster a mindset of strategic alignment at both parties. Start by asking, "If we were one company, how would we go to market differently?" and listen carefully to the responses. Implement these insights for your strategic relationship(s) and then replicate the approach for others, too.

We hope that you will go on to achieve great success in building lasting customer relationships and orchestrating mutual growth. Happy value creation!

NOTES

CHAPTER 1

1. With over 50 primary industry customers, Kotahi manages over 30% of New Zealand's containerized export volume. Kotahi, working with Maersk and other strategic partners, creates a sustainable and resilient supply chain for New Zealand exporters.

2. Henry Mintzberg, Bruce Ahlstrand, and Joseph Lampel *Strategy Safari: A Guided Tour through the Wilds of Strategic Management*, Simon and Schuster (2001); Maurizio Zollo, Mario Minoja, and Vittorio Coda, "Toward an Integrated Theory of Strategy," *Strategic Management Journal* 39, no. 6 (2018): 1753–1778.

3. George S. Yip, *Total Global Strategy* (Prentice Hall PTR, 2001); Michael D. Watkins, "Demystifying Strategy: The What, Who, How, and Why," *Harvard Business Review,* October 2007; Richard P. Rumelt, *Good Strategy/Bad Strategy: The Difference and Why it Matters* (New York: Crown Currency, 2011); R. P. Rumelt, "Good Strategy/ Bad Strategy: The Difference and Why it Matters," *Strategic Direction* 28, no. 8 (2012).

4. W. Chan Kim and Renée A. Mauborgne, *Blue Ocean Strategy, Expanded Edition: How to Create Uncontested Market Space and Make the Competition Irrelevant* (Boston: Harvard Business Review Press, 2014); Alexander Osterwalder and Yves Pigneur, *Business Model Generation: A Handbook for Visionaries, Game Changers, and Challengers,* Vol. 1 (Hoboken: John Wiley & Sons, 2010).

5. Noel Capon and Christoph Senn, "Customer-Centricity in the Executive Suite: A Taxonomy of Top-Management Customer Interaction Roles," in Pfeffermann N., Gould J. (eds.), *Strategy and Communication for Innovation* (2020), 165–176; Christoph Senn, "Stop Selling. Start Collaborating," *Harvard Business Review,* May–June 2022, 112–119.

6. Press Release, German Machine Tool Builders' Association (VDW), "Machine Tool Industry Expecting Decline in Production," January 22, 2024, https://vdw.de/en /Machine-tool-industry-expecting-decline-in-production/; *European Tool & Mould Making (ETMM) Magazine,* "German Machine Tool Industry Faces Challenges in 2023," November 14, 2023, https://www.etmm-online.com/german-machine-tool -industry-faces-challenges-in-2023-a-a114af46a9a9be71ccc04f89b28e688f/.

7. Christoph Senn, Axel Thoma, and George S. Yip, "Customer-Centric Leadership: How to Manage Strategic Customers as Assets in B2B Markets," *California Management Review* 55, no. 3 (2013): 27–59.

8. Matthew S. Olson, Derek van Bever, and Seth Verry, "When Growth Stalls," *Harvard Business Review*, March 2008, 50–61.

9. Reference for the Xerox case: George Day and Wharton Staff, "What Xerox Should Copy, and Not Copy, from Its Past," Knowledge at Wharton, October 25, 2000, https:// knowledge.wharton.upenn.edu/article/what-xerox-should-copy-and-not-copy-from-its -past/; Reference for the IBM case: James W. Cortada, "How the IBM PC Won, Then Lost, the Personal Computer Market," IEEE Spectrum, July 21, 2021, https://spectrum.ieee .org/how-the-ibm-pc-won-then-lost-the-personal-computer-market.

10. Adamantios Diamantopoulos, Bobo B. Schlegelmilch, and Johann P. Du Preez, "Lessons for Pan-European Marketing? The Role of Consumer Preferences in Fine- Tuning the Product-Market Fit," *International Marketing Review* 12, no. 2 (1995): 38–52; Marc Andreesen, "Product/Market Fit–EE204" Stanford University (2007), https:// web.stanford.edu/class/ee204/ProductMarketFit.html.

11. Heather Myers and Zasima Razack, "Validating Product-Market Fit in the Real World," *Harvard Business Review*, December 2022; Jeffrey Bussgang, "You Found Your Product-Market Fit. Now What?" hbr.org , July 30, 2013, https://hbr.org/2013/07 /three-ways-to-scale-b2b-sales.

12. Original customer quote in response to the value proposition pitch, Valuecreator research database.

13. Richard Wise and David Morrison, "Beyond the Exchange—The Future of B2B," *Harvard Business Review*, November–December 2000, 86–96.

14. Joona Keränen et al., "Advancing Value-Based Selling Research in B2B Markets," *Industrial Marketing Management* 111 (2023): 55–68; Sheila Mello, *Customer-Centric Product Definition: The Key to Great Product* (Charlottesville: PDC Professional Publishing, 2003); Andreas Hinterhuber, Todd C. Snelgrove, and Bo-Inge Stensson, "Value First, Then Price," *Journal of Revenue and Pricing Management* 20 (2021): 403– 409; Joona Keränen, Harri Terho, and Antti Saurama, "Three Ways to Sell Value in B2B Markets," *MIT Sloan Management Review* 63, no. 1 (2021).

15. Christoph Senn, "Stop Selling. Start Collaborating," *Harvard Business Review*, May–June 2022, 112–119; Christoph Senn, Axel Thoma, and George S. Yip, "Customer- Centric Leadership: How to Manage Strategic Customers as Assets in B2B Markets," *California Management Review* 55, no. 3 (2013): 27–59.

16. News references for the AgeCore cases with Nestle, AB InBev, Mars, PepsiCo, and Coca-Cola: Stefan Van Rompaey, "Agecore Increases the Pressure on Nestlé," April 6, 2018, RetailDetail, https://www.retaildetail.eu/news/food/agecore-increases -pressure-nestle/; Stefan Van Rompaey, "Analysis—Why Brands and Retailers are Quarrelling Over Purchasing Alliances," April 1, 2021, RetailDetail, https://www .retaildetail.eu/news/food/analysis-why-brands-and-retailers-are-quarrelling -over-buying-alliances/; Stefan Van Rompaey, "Agecore's War with Coca-Cola Spreads to Belgium," February 10, 2020, RetailDetail, https://www.retaildetail.eu/news/food /agecores-war-coca-cola-spreads-belgium/.

17. News references for the VW-Prevent case: Mike Scarcella, "VW Must Face Auto Parts Supplier Prevent's $750 Million Antitrust Lawsuit, US Judge Says," *Reuters*, August 4, 2023, https://www.reuters.com/legal/litigation/vw-must-face-auto-parts -supplier-prevents-750-mln-antitrust-lawsuit-us-judge-2023-08-04/; Marcus Williams, "VW Cancels Contracts with Prevent Group After Supply Problems," *Automotive Logistics*, April 10, 2018, https://www.automotivelogistics.media/vw -cancels-contracts-with-prevent-group-after-supply-problems/20561.article.

18. Peter F. Drucker, "New Society of Organizations," *Harvard Business Review*, September–October 1992, 281–293.

19. Peter Fader, *Customer Centricity: Focus on the Right Customers for Strategic Advantage* (Philadelphia: University of Pennsylvania Press, 2020); Nicolaj Siggelkow and Christian Terwiesch, *Connected Strategy: Building Continuous Customer Relationships for Competitive Advantage* (Boston: Harvard Business Review Press, 2019).

20. Freek Vermeulen, "Many Strategies Fail Because They're Not Actually Strategies," hbr.org, November 8, 2017, https://hbr.org/2017/11/many-strategies-fail -because-theyre-not-actually-strategies; Michael D. Watkins, "Demystifying Strategy: The What, Who, How, and Why," hbr.org, September 10, 2007; Richard Rumelt, "The Perils of Bad Strategy," *McKinsey Quarterly* 1, no. 3 (2011): 1–10; Jim Tincher, *Do B2B Better: Drive Growth through Game-Changing Customer Experience* (Los Angeles: LifeTree Media, 2022); Nick Toman, Brent Adamson, and Cristina Gomez, "The New Sales Imperative," *Harvard Business Review*, March–April 2017, 118–125.

21. Alan Pennington, *The Customer Experience Manual: How to Design, Measure and Improve Customer Experience in Your Business* (London: Pearson UK, 2016).

22. Vijay Govindarajan and Venkat Venkatraman, "The Next Great Digital Advantage," *Harvard Business Review*, May–June 2022, 55–56.

23. "B2B eCommerce - In-depth Market Insights & Data Analysis," Statista (2024): https://www.statista.com/markets/413/topic/458/b2b-e-commerce/#insights; https://www.statista.com/study/44442/in-depth-report-b2b-e-commerce/.

24. Paul Hague and Nicholas Hague, *B2B Customer Experience: A Practical Guide to Delivering Exceptional CX* (London: Kogan Page Publishers, 2023).

25. Arianne Walker, "Amazon and Stellantis Collaborate to Introduce Customer-Centric Connected Experiences Across Millions of Vehicles, Helping Accelerate Stellantis' Software Transformation," Press Release, Amazon.com Developer Blog, January 5, 2022, https://developer.amazon.com/en-US/blogs/alexa/alexa-auto/2022 /01/amazon-and-stellantis-collaborate-to-introduce-customer-centric-.

26. "Announcing the New AWS Secret Region," AWS Public Sector Blog, November 20, 2017, https://aws.amazon.com/de/blogs/publicsector/announcing-the-new-aws -secret-region/.

27. Collaborative Customer Relationships (CCR) consortium results (2018–2021), Valuecreator research database.

28. Russell L. Ackoff, "On the Use of Models in Corporate Planning," *Strategic Management Journal* 2, no. 4 (1981): 353–359.

29. Value creation projects conducted with Microsoft account managers (2012–2014), Valuecreator research database.

30. Microsoft keynote at Value Creation Summit 2023, Valuecreator research database.

CHAPTER 2

1. Christoph Senn, "Stop Selling. Start Collaborating," *Harvard Business Review*, May–June 2022, 112–119.

2. Harvard Business School Press, *Harvard Business Review on Advances in Strategy* (Boston: Harvard Business Review Press, 2002).

3. Christoph Senn, Axel Thoma, and George S. Yip, "Customer-Centric Leadership: How to Manage Strategic Customers as Assets in B2B Markets," *California Management Review* 55, no. 3 (2013): 27–59.

4. Alaric Bourgoin, Francois Marchessaux, and Nicolas Bencherki, "We Need to Talk about Strategy: How to Conduct Effective Strategic Dialogue," *Business Horizons* 61, no. 4 (2018): 87–97.

5. Harvard Business Review, *Harvard Business Review on Strategies for Growth* (Boston: Harvard Business School Press, 1998).

6. Satoshi Hino, *Inside the Mind of Toyota: Management Principles for Enduring Growth* (Boca Raton, FL: CRC Press, 2005); Samuel Obara and Darril Wilburn, *Toyota by Toyota: Reflections from the Inside Leaders on the Techniques That Revolutionized the Industry* (Boca Raton, FL: CRC Press, 2012); Mark Rodgers and Rosa Oppenheim, "Ishikawa Diagrams and Bayesian Belief Networks for Continuous Improvement Applications," *TQM Journal* 31, no. 3 (2019): 294–318.

7. Jeffrey Liker, *Toyota Way: 14 Management Principles from the World's Greatest Manufacturer* (New York: McGraw-Hill Education, 2021).

8. Personal conversation with Michael Dobler, Valuecreator research database.

9. Annie H. Liu, Mark P. Leach, and Richa Chugh, "A Sales Process Framework to Regain B2B Customers," *Journal of Business & Industrial Marketing* 30, no. 8 (2015): 906–914; Oskar Lingqvist, Candace Lun Plotkin, and Jennifer Stanley, "Do You Really Understand How Your Business Customers Buy," *McKinsey Quarterly* 1 (2015): 74–85.

CHAPTER 3

1. Freek Vermeulen, "Many Strategies Fail Because They're Not Actually Strategies," hbr.org, November 8, 2017.

2. Donald Sull, Rebecca Homkes, and Charles Sull, "Why Strategy Execution Unravels—and What to Do about It," *Harvard Business Review*, March 2015, 57–66; Gary L. Neilson, Karla L. Martin, and Elizabeth Powers, "The Secrets to Successful Strategy Execution," *Harvard Business Review*, June 2008; Eucman Lee and Phanish Puranam, "The Implementation Imperative: Why One Should Implement Even Imperfect Strategies Perfectly," *Strategic Management Journal* 37, no. 8 (2016): 1529–1546; Chris McChesney, Sean Covey, and Jim Huling, *The 4 Disciplines of Execution: Achieving Your Wildly Important Goals* (New York: Simon and Schuster, 2012).

3. European Commission, "Reform of the EU Statutory Audit Market," press release, June 17, 2016, https://ec.europa.eu/commission/presscorner/detail/en/MEMO_16_2244.

CHAPTER 4

1. Alan Weinstein, presentation, University of St. Gallen, GAM Forum, October 2019, Valuecreator research database.

2. Press Release, BASF, "BASF Wins 3M for the Supplier of the Year Award" (2021), https://www.basf.com/us/en/media/news-releases/2021/02/basf-wins-3m-2020-supplier-of-the-year-award.html.

3. Personal conversations during coaching sessions with the BASF-Natura team (2022–2024), Valuecreator internal database.

4. Gary P. Pisano, "How Fast Should Your Company Really Grow?" *Harvard Business Review*, March–April 2024, 39–45.

5. Paul Saffo, "Six Rules for Effective Forecasting," *Harvard Business Review*, July–August 2007, 122.

6. Alexander Dierks et al., "Leveraging Growth Analytics for B2B Sales," hbr.org, March 21, 2023, https://hbr.org/2023/03/leveraging-growth-analytics-for-b2b-sales; Heli Hallikainen, Emma Savimäki, and Tommi Laukkanen, "Fostering B2B Sales with Customer Big Data Analytics," *Industrial Marketing Management* 86 (2020): 90–98; Jiwat Ram and Zeyang Zhang, "Examining the Needs to Adopt Big Data Analytics

in B2B Organizations: Development of Propositions and Model of Needs," *Journal of Business & Industrial Marketing* 37, no. 4 (2022): 790–809; Michael A. Cusumano, Steven J. Kahl, and Fernando F. Suarez, "Services, Industry Evolution, and the Competitive Strategies of Product Firms," *Strategic Management Journal* 36, no. 4 (2015): 559–575.

7. The research consortia were conducted over the period of 25 years (from 1998 to 2024), first under the direction of Christoph Senn and later together with Mehak Gandhi in the following sequence:

1. MGC Consortium (1998–1999), University of St. Gallen.
2. GBM Consortium (1998–2000), University of St. Gallen.
3. MEGA Consortium (1999–2000), University of St. Gallen.
4. MCI Consortium (2000–2001), University of St. Gallen.
5. GAMBIT I Consortium (2002–2003), University of St. Gallen.
6. GAMBIT II Consortium (2004–2005), University of St. Gallen and Columbia Business School.
7. CSI Consortium (2006–2009), Columbia Business School.
8. GAM Forum (2010–2011), Columbia Business School.
9. CCR Consortium (2018–2022), University of St. Gallen.
10. BBR Consortium (2023–2024), INSEAD.

8. Mehak Gandhi, "From Value Selling to Value Co-Creation: Understanding the Key Elements of Value Co-Creation between Suppliers and Customers," 4th Industrial Marketing Management Summit, January 28, 2021, Copenhagen; Mehak Gandhi, "Navigating B2B Relationships in Uncertain Times: Five Strategic Choices to Enhance B2B Collaboration," European Marketing Conference, May 26, 2021, Bucharest; Mehak Gandhi, "Is Your Corporate Strategy Truly Customer-Centric? How to Add Corporate Alignment to Customer Account Plans," European Marketing Conference, May 25, 2022, Budapest.

9. "Evonik Opens New $768M Methionine Plant on Jurong Island," Singapore Economic Development Board (EDB) Press Release, June 18, 2019, https://www.edb.gov.sg/en/about-edb/media-releases-publications/evonik-opens-new-768m-methionine-plant-on-jurong-island.html#.

10. "Expansion of Evonik's DL-Methionine Production Capacity in Singapore Moves to Next Stage," Evonik Corporate Press Release, July 25, 2023, https://corporate.evonik.com/en/investor-relations/expansion-of-evoniks-dl-methionine-production-capacity-in-singapore-moves-to-next-stage-211675.html.

CHAPTER 5

1. Grupo Peñaflor, "Who We Are," https://grupopenaflor.com.ar/en/who-we-are.
2. Andy Bacon, "Strategic Account-Based Marketing: How to Tame This Beast," in *B2B Marketing: A Guidebook for the Classroom to the Boardroom* (Berlin: Springer International Publishing, 2021), 419–435; Varun Kohli, Ryan Paulowsky, and Jennifer Stanley, "How Digital Is Powering the Next Wave of Growth in Key-Account Management," McKinsey & Company, 2019; Boudewijn Driedonks and Ryan Paulowsky, "Two Ingredients for Successful B2B Sales: Agility and Stability," 2021, https://www.mckinsey.com/capabilities/growth-marketing-and-sales/our-insights/two-ingredients-for-successful-b2b-sales-agility-and-stability.
3. Jose R. Saura, Domingo Ribeiro-Soriano, and Daniel Palacios-Marqués, "Setting B2B Digital Marketing in Artificial Intelligence-Based CRMs: A Review and Directions for Future Research," *Industrial Marketing Management* 98 (2021): 161–178.

4. Roger L. Martin, "The Big Lie of Strategic Planning," *Harvard Business Review*, January–February 2014, 78–84; Michael Mankins and Richard Steele, "Stop Making Plans; Start Making Decisions," *Harvard Business Review*, January 2006, 76–84.

5. Annual surveys with key account managers attending our executive education programs, Valuecreator research database.

6. Boudewijn Driedonks and Ryan Paulowsky, "Two Ingredients for Successful B2B Sales: Agility and Stability," McKinsey Research; Simon Hall, *B2B Digital Marketing Strategy: How to Use New Frameworks and Models to Achieve Growth* (London: Kogan Page Publishers, 2023); Sean Geehan, *B2B Executive Playbook: The Ultimate Weapon for Achieving Sustainable, Predictable and Profitable Growth* (Covington, KY: Clerisy Press, 2011).

7. Christoph Senn, "Stop Selling. Start Collaborating," *Harvard Business Review*, May–June 2022; N. Piercy and N. Lane, "The Underlying Vulnerabilities in Key Account Management Strategies," *European Management Journal* 24, no. 2–3 (2006): 151–162; Daniel D. Prior, *B2B Customer Engagement Strategy: An Introduction to Managing Customer Experience* (Berlin: Springer Nature, 2023); Simon Hall, *B2B Digital Marketing Strategy.*

8. Roger L. Martin, "Don't Let Strategy Become Planning," hbr.org, February 5, 2013, https://hbr.org/2013/02/dont-let-strategy-become-plann.

9. Brian Gregg et al., "Rapid Revenue Recovery: A Road Map for Post-Covid-19 Growth," *McKinsey Digital,* www.mckinsey. com/businessfunctions/marketing-and -sales/our-insights/rapid-revenue-recovery-a-road-map-for-post-COVID-19-growth (accessed May 14, 2020).

10. Abraham Grosfeld-Nir, Boaz Ronen, and Nir Kozlovsky, "The Pareto Managerial Principle: When Does It Apply?" *International Journal of Production Research* 45, no. 10 (2007): 2317–2325; R. Dunford, Q. Su, and E. Tamang, "The Pareto Principle," *The Plymouth Student Scientist* 7, no. 1 (2014); J. Sutherland and D. Canwell "Pareto Principle," (2004); J. Backhaus, "The Pareto Principle," *Analyse & Kritik* 2, no. 2 (1980); 146–171.

11. Frank V. Cespedes and León Poblete, "How B2B Companies Can Win Back Customers They've Lost," hbr.org, June 3, 2019, https://hbr.org/2019/06/how-b2b -companies-can-win-back-customers-theyve-lost.

12. Marta Giovannetti et al., "Understanding the Enduring Shifts in Sales Strategy and Processes Caused by the Covid-19 Pandemic," *Journal of Business & Industrial Marketing* (2023).

13. Amau Bages-Amat et al., "These Eight Charts Show How Covid-19 Changed B2B Sales Forever," McKinsey, October 14, 2020, https://www.mckinsey.com/capabilities /growth-marketing-and-sales/our-insights/these-eight-charts-show-how-covid-19 -has-changed-b2b-sales-forever.

14. The concept of presenting the key idea first backed up by supporting arguments has been introduced by Barbara Minto in her seminal book *The Pyramid Principle*, first published in 1999 and later revised in 2009. If you are interested in a hands-on instruction of delivering great business presentations, we highly recommend this book as further reading.

CHAPTER 6

1. Michele Bertoncello et al., "Unlocking the Full Life-Cycle Value from Connected-Car Data," *McKinsey,* February 2021; Michael Chui, Mark Collins, and Mark Patel, "The Internet of Things: Catching Up to an Accelerating Opportunity," 2021, McKinsey Research; Vodafone, "3.3 Billion Devices Will Be Trading with Each

Other by 2030 According to New Report," Technology News, June 1, 2023, https://www
.vodafone.com/news/technology/3-3-billion-devices-trading-2030-report.

2. Lawrence G. Hrebiniak, *Making Strategy Work: Leading Effective Execution and Change* (Upper Saddle River, NJ: Financial Times Press, 2013).

3. Paul Hong, Sandeep Jagani, Phuoc Pham, and Euisung Jung, "Globalization Orientation, Business Practices and Performance Outcomes: An Empirical Investigation of B2B Manufacturing Firms," *Journal of Business & Industrial Marketing* 38, no. 10 (2023): 2259–2274.

4. John C. Camillus, "Strategy as a Wicked Problem," *Harvard Business Review*, May 2008, 98–101; Edward H. Bowman and Constance E. Helfat, "Does Corporate Strategy Matter?," *Strategic Management Journal* 22, no. 1 (2001): 1–23.

5. Emilie R. Feldman, "Corporate Strategy: Past, Present, and Future," 2005; Markus Baer, Kurt T. Dirks, and Jackson A. Nickerson, "Microfoundations of Strategic Problem Formulation," *Strategic Management Journal* 34, no. 2 (2013): 197–214; C. Chet Miller and Laura B. Cardinal, "Strategic Planning and Firm Performance," in *The Psychology of Planning in Organizations. Research and Applications* (New York: Routledge, 2015), 260–288; Jane E. Dutton and Robert B. Duncan, "The Influence of the Strategic Planning Process on Strategic Change," *Strategic Management Journal* 8, no. 2 (1987): 103–116; Renée Dye and Olivier Sibony, "How to Improve Strategic Planning," *McKinsey Quarterly* 3 (2007): 40; Carola Wolf and Steven W. Floyd, "Strategic Planning Research: Toward a Theory-Driven Agenda," *Journal of Management* 43, no. 6 (2017): 1754–1788.

6. Michael Mankins and Richard Steele, "Stop Making Plans; Start Making Decisions," *Harvard Business Review*, January 2006, 76–84; Robert M. Grant, "The Knowledge-Based View of the Firm," *The Oxford Handbook of Strategy: A Strategy Overview and Competitive Strategy* (New York: Oxford University Press, 2006), 203–230.

7. Rodrigo Guesalaga and Wesley Johnston, "What's Next in Key Account Management Research? Building the Bridge between the Academic Literature and the Practitioners' Priorities," *Industrial Marketing Management* 39, no. 7 (2010): 1063–1068.

8. Noel Capon and Christoph Senn, "When CEOs Make Sales Calls," *Harvard Business Review*, March–April 2021.

9. Ranjay Gulati, *Reorganize for Resilience: Putting Customers at the Center of Your Business* (Boston: Harvard Business Press, 2010); Ranjay Gulati, "Silo Busting: How to Execute on the Promise of Customer Focus," *Harvard Business Review*, May 2007, 98–108; Gillian Tett, *The Silo Effect: Why Putting Everything in Its Place Isn't Such a Bright Idea* (London: Hachette UK, 2015).

10. Aaron J. Shenhar et al., "Linking Project Management to Business Strategy," Project Management Institute, September 2007; Christian Schrader, Juergen Freimann, and Stefan Seuring, "Business Strategy at the Base of the Pyramid," *Business Strategy and the Environment* 21, no. 5 (2012): 281–298; Paul C. Dinsmore and Terence J. Cooke-Davies, *Right Projects Done Right: From Business Strategy to Successful Project Implementation* (New York: John Wiley & Sons, 2005); Turki Alsudiri, Wafi Al-Karaghouli, and Tillal Eldabi, "Alignment of Large Project Management Process to Business Strategy," *Journal of Enterprise Information Management* 26, no. 5 (2013): 596–615; Andrew Longman and James Mullins, "Project Management: Key Tool for Implementing Strategy," *Journal of Business Strategy* 25, no. 5 (2004): 54–60; Trevor L. Young, *Successful Project Management* (London: Kogan Page Publishers, 2016); Arun Sharma, R. Krishnan, and Dhruv Grewal, "Value Creation in Markets: A Critical Area of Focus for Business-to-Business Markets," *Industrial Marketing Management* 30, no. 4 (2001): 391–402.

11. Carina Loiro et al., "Agile Project Management: A Communicational Workflow Proposal," *Procedia Computer Science* 164 (2018): 485–490; Mirjam Minor, Alexander Tartakovski, and Daniel Schmalen, "Agile Workflow Technology and Case-Based Change Reuse for Long-Term Processes," *International Journal of Intelligent Information Technologies* 4, no. 1 (2008): 80–98.

CHAPTER 7

1. Jeffrey A. Ogden, "Supply Base Reduction: An Empirical Study of Critical Success Factors," *Journal of Supply Chain Management: A Global Review of Purchasing and Supply* 42, no. 4 (November 2006): 30–40; Ashutosh Sarkar and Pratap Mohapatra, "Evaluation of Supplier Capability and Performance: A Method for Supply Base Reduction," *Journal of Purchasing and Supply Management* 12, no. 3 (May 2006): 148–163; Jagdish N. Sheth and Arun Sharma, "Supplier Relationships: Emerging Issues and Challenges," *Industrial Marketing Management* 26, no. 2 (March 1997): 91–100.

2. P&G Annual Report 2023, Part I, Business Risks—Key Customers, page 1, https://assets.ctfassets.net/oggad6svuzkv/2pIQQWQXPpxiKjjmhfpyWf /eb17b3f3c9c21f7abb05e68c7b1f3fcd/2023_annual_report.pdf.

3. Gail McGovern et al., "Bringing Customers into the Boardroom," *Harvard Business Review,* November 2004, 70–80; Sunil Gupta and Donald Lehmann, *Managing Customers as Investments: The Strategic Value of Customers in the Long Run* (Upper Saddle River, NJ: Pearson, 2005); Lynette Ryals and Simon Knox, "Measuring and Managing Customer Relationship Risk in Business Markets," *Industrial Marketing Management* 36, no. 6 (August 2007): 823–833.

4. Christoph Senn, Axel Thoma, and George S. Yip, "Customer-Centric Leadership—Who's Managing Your Customer Assets?," *California Management Review* 55, no. 3 (Spring 2013): 27–59.

5. Benson Honig, "Learning Strategies and Resources for Entrepreneurs and Intrapreneurs," *Entrepreneurship Theory and Practice* 26, no. 1 (2001): 21–34; Rolf Wunderer, "Employees as 'Co-Intrapreneurs'—A Transformation Concept," *Leadership & Organization Development Journal* 22, no. 5 (2001): 193–211.

6. W. Chan Kim, and Renée A. Mauborgne, *Blue Ocean Strategy, Expanded Edition: How to Create Uncontested Market Space and Make the Competition Irrelevant* (Boston: Harvard Business Review Press, 2014).

7. Ross Brennan, Louise Canning, and Ray McDowell, "Price-Setting in Business-to-Business Markets," *The Marketing Review* 7, no. 3 (2007): 207–234; Tingtin Christina Zhang, Melissa Farboudi Jahromi, and Murat Kizildag, "Value Co-Creation in a Sharing Economy: The End of Price Wars?," *International Journal of Hospitality Management* 71 (2018): 51–58; Michael Bungert, *Termination of Price Wars: A Signaling Approach* (Berlin: Springer Science & Business Media, 2012).

8. George Tobias et al., "Sellers Are Overwhelmed by New Technology," hbr.org, August 22, 2023; Jean-Claude Larreche, *Value Capture Selling: How to Win the 3rd Sales Transformation* (Hoboken, NJ: Wiley, 2023).

9. Presentation by Patrice Spinner in Christoph's MBA courses at Columbia Business School, 2003–2012, Valuecreator research database; Sallie Sherman, Joseph Sperry, and Samuel Reese, *The Seven Keys to Managing Strategic Accounts* (New York: McGraw Hill, 2003).

10. James K. Sebenius and Ellen Knebel, *Tom Muccio: Negotiating the P & G Relationship with Wal-Mart (A)*, Harvard Business School, 2007; Sarah Nassauer and Sharon Terlep, "Wal-mart and P&G: A $10 Billion Marriage under Strain," *The Wall Street Journal,* June 14, 2016, https://www.wsj.com/articles/wal-mart-and-p-g-a-10

-billion-marriage-under-strain-1465948431; Tom Muccio, *Collaborative Disruption— The Walmart and P&G Partnership That Changed Retail Forever* (unpublished manuscript, May 7, 2024).

11. Keynote presentation by Tom Muccio at the Value Creation Summit, September 22, 2017, in Arbon, Switzerland.

12. Sarah Nassauer and Sharon Terlep, "Wal-Mart and P&G: A $10 Billion Marriage under Strain," *Wall Street Journal,* June 14, 2016, https://www.wsj.com/articles/wal -mart-and-p-g-a-10-billion-marriage-under-strain-1465948431.

13. P&G Annual Report 2023, p. 12, Key Customers: "Sales to Walmart Inc. and its affiliates represent approximately 15% of our total sales in 2023, 2022 and 2021. No other customer represents more than 10% of our total sales."

CHAPTER 8

1. Personal conversation with the responsible global account manager and team at the supplier firm.

2. Personal conversation with a Merck procurement executive, Valuecreator research database.

3. See, for example, Christian Homburg, John P. Workman, and Ove Jensen, "A Configurational Perspective on Key Account Management," *Journal of Marketing* 66 (April 2002): 38–60; and John P. Workman, Christian Homburg, and Ove Jensen, "Intra-organizational Determinants of Key Account Management Effectiveness," *Journal of the Academy of Marketing Science* 31, no. 1 (2003): 3–21; Noel Capon and Christoph Senn, "Global Customer Programs: How to Make Them Really Work," *California Management Review* 52, no. 2 (Winter 2010): 32–55.

4. For instance, see A.G. Lafley, "What Only the CEO Can Do," *Harvard Business Review,* May 2009, 54–62; Christoph Senn, "The Executive Growth Factor—How Siemens Invigorated Its Customer Relationships," *Journal of Business Strategy* 27, no. 1 (2006): 27–34; John Quelch, "How CEO's Should Work with Customers," *Harvard Business Review* (blog), September 22, 2008, http://blogs.hbr.org/2008/09 /how-ceos-should-work-with-cust/.

5. Michael E. Porter and Nitin Nohria, "How CEOs Manage Their Time" and "What Do CEOs Actually Do?," *Harvard Business Review,* July–August 2018.

6. Analyzing 311 studies of interaction behaviors in B2B relationships, Guercini, La Rocca, Runfola, and Snehota state: "[M]ost of the research on interaction in business relationships appears to 'black-box' individual interaction behaviors. . . . There are relatively few empirically oriented papers."; Simone Guercini et al., "Interaction Behaviors in Business Relationships and Heuristics: Issues for Management and Research Agenda," *Industrial Marketing Management* 43, no. 6 (2014): 929–937.

7. Rodrigo Guesalaga and Wesley Johnston, "What's Next in Key Account Management Research? Building the Bridge between the Academic Literature and the Practitioners' Priorities," *Industrial Marketing Management* 39, no. 7 (2010): 1063-1068; Linda Hui Shi et al., "Executive Insights: Global Account Management Capability: Insights from Leading Suppliers," *Journal of International Marketing* 13, no. 2 (2005): 93–113; Lawrence Bossidy and Ram Charan, *Execution: The Discipline of Getting Things Done* (New York, Crown Business, 2002). For a further overview, see: Ajay K. Kohli and Bernard J. Jaworski, "Market Orientation: The Construct, Research Propositions and Managerial Implications," *Journal of Marketing* 54, no. 2 (1990): 1–18; Bernard J. Jaworski and Ajay K. Kohli, "Market Orientation: Antecedents and Consequences," *Journal of Marketing* 57, no. 3 (1993): 53–70; Stanley F. Slater and John C. Narver, "Market Orientation and the Learning Organization," *Journal of Marketing* 59, no. 3 (1995): 63–74;

Christian Homburg, John P. Workman, and Ove Jensen, "Fundamental Changes in Marketing Organization: The Movement toward a Customer-Focused Organizational Structure," *Journal of the Academy of Marketing Science* 28, no. 4 (2000): 459–478; George S. Day, "Aligning the Organization with the Market," *MIT Sloan Management Review* 48, no. 1 (2006): 41–49.

8. Correspondingly, Håkannsson and Waluszewski conclude: "We have to find much more precise ways to describe, characterize and analyze single interactions as well as patterns of interaction." Håkan Håkansson and Alexandra Waluszewski, "A Never Ending Story—Interaction Patterns and Economic Development," *Industrial Marketing Management* 42, no. 3 (2013): 443–454.

9. Jerry R. Goolsby, "A Theory of Role Stress in Boundary Spanning Positions of Marketing Organizations," *Journal of the Academy of Marketing Science* 20, no. 2 (1992): 155–164.

10. Personal conversation with the responsible account manager.

11. Noel Capon and Christoph Senn, "When CEOs Make Sales Calls," *Harvard Business Review*, March–April 2021.

12. Keynote by Franz Speer at St. Gallen GAM Executive Program, 2013.

13. Edward O'Donnell, Steven Brown, and Laurence Marsh, "To Commit or Not to Commit? The Influence of Relationships Governance on Buyer-Seller Commitment," *Academy of Marketing Studies Journal* 18, no. 1 (2014): 87–98; Sandy D. Jap, "Pie-Expansion Efforts: Collaboration Processes in Buyer-Seller Relationships," *Journal of Marketing Research* 36, no. 4 (1999): 461–475.

CHAPTER 9

1. Valuecreator research database.

2. Emily Rose McRae et al., "9 Trends That Will Shape Work in 2023 and Beyond," hbr.org, January 18, 2023, https://hbr.org/2023/01/9-trends-that-will-shape-work-in-2023-and-beyond.

3. John P. Kotter, *Leading Change: Why Transformation Efforts Fail* (Boston: Harvard Business Review Press, 2007, rev. 2012).

4. Attributed to P. Drucker as stated in Stephen B. Tallman, Oded Shenkar, and Jie Wu, "'Culture Eats Strategy for Breakfast': Use and Abuse of Culture in International Strategy Research," *Strategic Management Review* (2021).

5. Emily Field, Elizabeth Pears, and Bill Schaninger, "A Single Approach to Culture Transformation May Not Fit All," McKinsey, 2022 https://www.mckinsey.com/capabilities/people-and-organizational-performance/our-insights/a-single-approach-to-culture-transformation-may-not-fit-all.

6. Heike Bruch and Sumantra Ghoshal, "Beware the Busy Manager," *Harvard Business Review*, February 2002, 62–69; Heike Bruch and Sumantra Ghoshal, *A Bias for Action: How Effective Managers Harness Their Willpower, Achieve Results, and Stop Wasting Time* (Boston: Harvard Business Press, 2004).

7. Aaron De Smet, Chris Gagnon, and Elizabeth Mygatt, "Organizing for the Future: Nine Keys to Becoming a Future-Ready Company," *McKinsey*, January 11, 2021.

8. Paul Meehan, Orit Gadiesh, and Shintaro Hori, "Culture as Competitive Advantage," *Leader to Leader* 2006, no. 39 (2006): 55–61; C. Marlene Fio, "Managing Culture as a Competitive Resource: An Identity-Based View of Sustainable Competitive Advantage," *Journal of Management* 17, no. 1 (1991): 191–211.

INDEX

ACKNOWLEDGMENTS

Most authors would probably agree that the hardest part of writing—is writing. And we are no exception to this experience. But our constant exposure to real-life business challenges has inspired us to generalize best practices and experiences into a written format so that they can benefit many readers across industries. The results from our consulting, training, and research work has provided solid evidence for all the frameworks and tools presented in this book. Furthermore, the ongoing encouragement from our global community has motivated us to persevere through the validation and sharing of their stories. We are grateful to acknowledge the tremendous support along this journey that has finally made this book possible.

First and foremost, we would like to thank all the business leaders who believed in our work to help them create value beyond products. Collaborating with all of you over the past twenty-five years was (and still is) a priceless privilege we treasure deeply. There is not enough space to list all our connections, especially with the people and companies featured in this book—but we would like to thank every one of you. We would like to emphasize the exceptional support from Jihane Achkar, Michel Belland, Celia Belline, Jens Böhm, Vincent Clerc, Michael Dobler, Nicholas Guthier, René Janesch, Michael Heuer, Niels Hougaard, Detlev Lindner, Matthias Kiessling, Heinz Kundert,

Daijirou Morinaga, Manuel Müller, Francois Pourprix, Niels Pörksen, Yves Rogivue, David Ross, Parand Salmassinia, Cyrill Salzmann, Christoph Solenthaler, Joern Taubert, Sanjay Vasudevan, Matthias Wolfgruber, and Anne Witte. May your leadership as growth champions inspire countless others.

Second, we owe a huge thanks to the team at Harvard Business School Press. Scott Berinato, you were not only our trusted adviser and editor for both writing and visualizing, but also a rock-solid source of hope when our writing needed a course correction. Your continuous feedback on our often roughly developed ideas was instrumental in accomplishing this book. Thank you Dan McGinn and Juan Martinez for guiding us in our journey as first-time authors, and Victoria Desmond and Jane Gebhart for polishing our book manuscript in a way we could never have done. Your advice and contributions were pivotal in making this book a success.

Third, we would like to acknowledge the great help we had from our team at Valuecreator: Peter Andersson, Christian Doganer, Christian Loewe, Piotr Malita, Nicolaas Smit, and Ernst Zollinger for coaching many of the projects featured in this book, and Sam Schoeb and Michelle Senn for marketing and event support. Your encouragement and belief in our work fueled our determination to continue the journey despite all the challenges and search for value beyond products. A special thanks to Christophor Jenni for his contribution to the Triple Fit concept discussions, project coaching, and his relentless efforts to transform Triple Fit tools into a robust digital platform. We are grateful to acknowledge the longtime collaboration with Noel Capon from Columbia Business School, George Yip from Imperial College, and Heike Bruch, Rolf Dubs, Simon Evenett, Martin Hilb, Thomas Rudolph, Winfried Ruigrok, Roger Moser, Axel Thoma, Thorsten Truijens, and Andreas Wittmer during our time at the University of St. Gallen. We also owe a big thanks to Thomas Bechter, Nana von Bernuth, Sigrid Brendel, Frank Cespedes, David Cummins, Melanie Gabriel, Marco Hilty, Tom Muccio, Rainer Stern, and Alex Zwyer, who provided valuable feedback on our manuscript.

Fourth, we are grateful for the support from INSEAD in many ways. We are thankful for the collaboration with the INSEAD Marketing and Sales Excellence Initiative (MSEI) team with Wolfgang Ulaga, Wai Yee Fong, and Marie Drunat. We also owe many thanks to INSEAD's leadership with Lily Fang, dean of research; Ben Bensaou and Sameer Hasija, deans of executive education; Laurence Capron and Javier Gimeno, deans of faculty; and W. Chan Kim, Jay Kim, Nathalie Nawrocki, Karthik Rajaraman, and Chris Donaldson for their feedback and for allowing us to test and refine our concepts and frameworks during teaching assignments at INSEAD's global campus network in executive education classes and internal seminars.

Finally, and most importantly, we would like to thank the real heroes of this book—the thousands of account managers and their teams who participated in Triple Fit programs, trainings, events, and workshops worldwide. We would especially like to thank Jens Andresen, Olivier Aubertin, René Brulc, Lars Blank Schmeltzer, Patricia Cavalheri, Sharon E. Clemons, Line Ann Corfixen, Christine Dickson, Stephan Deichstetter, Josefina Godoy Lemos, Thayza Guimaraes, Martin Greuter, Ariane Helmbrecht, Mark Heil, Virginie Jackson, Ralph Koehler, Sue Lawson, Ho Sung Lee, Moshe Loberant, Fabiane Martins, Miro Milojkovic, Ernst Padrun, Juliana Polizel, Sven Rau, Goede Schueler, Nicolas Seegmüller, Konrad Schmid, Keith Shaw, Lars Tacke, Andrew Uasike, Victor Walzberg, Michael Weller, and Alan Weinstein. This book wouldn't have been possible without your constant efforts to orchestrate value creation. The business relationship challenges and real-life customer stories you shared have inspired us to develop and refine the tools that support your daily hard work and successfully apply Triple Fit strategies in your respective industries. We hope you will continue to make joint growth with customers your mission. May this journey never stop!

ABOUT THE AUTHORS

CHRISTOPH SENN helps individuals and organizations build lasting business relationships. He is an adjunct professor of marketing at INSEAD and codirector of INSEAD's Marketing and Sales Excellence Initiative (MSEI), in Fontainebleau, France. Before joining academia, Christoph held international sales and marketing roles in a high-tech company. After his time in industry, he founded Valuecreator, a global provider of growth tools and programs dedicated to advancing the practice of value creation across industries. He is the inventor of the Triple Fit Canvas, a sales framework designed to facilitate collaboration between sellers and buyers with a 360-degree perspective on business relationships.

Initially trained as a primary school teacher, Christoph received a master's degree, a doctoral degree (summa cum laude), and a Habilitation (Venia Legendi) from the University of St. Gallen, Switzerland. Prior to joining INSEAD, he taught at the University of St. Gallen, Columbia Business School in New York, Rotterdam School of Management in the Netherlands, and the Technical University of Hamburg-Harburg, Germany, and has won several teaching and research awards. He has published his work in journals such as the *California Management Review, Harvard Business Review, Industrial Marketing Management, Research Technology Management,* the *Wall Street Journal* and others.

In his public service, Christoph retired as Lieutenant-Colonel General Staff in the Swiss Army after serving as Commander of a Mechanized Infantry Battalion in the Swiss Army. He is also president of St. Gallen Oncology Conferences, a nonprofit foundation dedicated to distributing knowledge for health-care professionals caring for cancer patients at the national and international levels, to promote the implementation of research-based knowledge and to advance cancer care in clinical practice.

MEHAK GANDHI helps companies design next-generation sales organizations. She is the head of research and training at Valuecreator, Switzerland. Her work is focused on advancing B2B collaboration strategies and executing consulting projects and training programs to help companies accelerate growth with their strategic customers through the Triple Fit tools and research insights. She has supported several leading global companies including Allianz, Evonik, Konica Minolta, Maersk, Otis, Schindler, Schneider Electric, Sonos, Südzucker Group, Thermo Fisher, VAT, and WMF/Schaerer.

She received her doctoral degree in management (cum laude) from the University of St. Gallen, Switzerland, for her dissertation titled "The Dynamics of Successful Collaboration in B2B Relationships: Strategies and Best Practices from Global Firms." She also holds a second Swiss degree, the *Financial Times* top-ranked master of arts (in strategy and international management), from the University of St. Gallen.

Prior to Valuecreator AG, she worked at the Research Institute for International Management at the University of St. Gallen, where she was responsible for the design and delivery of executive education programs for the erstwhile Competence Center for Global Account Management, managing more than 350 value creation projects from global participants representing over 40 nationalities and companies across multiple industries during her tenure.

She also holds a bachelor's degree in mathematics from the University of Delhi, India, and worked with Tata Group and Deutsche Bank in India before moving to Switzerland, where she currently resides.